Raising Your
Kids to Be
Sexually Pure

"A practical answer to a real problem . . ."
—Jack W. Hayford

Raising Your Kids to Be Sexually Pure

Richard & Renée Durfield

SPIRE

© 2004 by Richard and Renée Durfield

Published by Fleming H. Revell
a division of Baker Publishing Group
P.O. Box 6287, Grand Rapids, MI 49516-6287
www.revellbooks.com

Spire edition published 2007
ISBN 10: 0-8007-8756-0
ISBN 978-0-8007-8756-1

Previously published in 2004 under the title *Raising Pure Kids In an Impure World* by
Bethany House Publishers

Parts of chapter 2 first appeared as "A Promise With a Ring to It" by Richard Durfield in
the April 1990 issue of *Focus on the Family* magazine. Used by permission.

Printed in the United States of America

Unless otherwise indicated, Scripture is taken from the King James Version of the
Bible.

Scripture marked NIV is taken from the HOLY BIBLE, NEW INTERNATIONAL
VERSION®. NIV®. Copyright © 1973, 1978, 1984 by International Bible Society.
Used by permission of Zondervan. All rights reserved.

Scripture marked NASB is taken from the New American Standard Bible®, Copyright ©
1960, 1962, 1963, 1968, 1971, 1972, 1973, 1975, 1977, 1995 by The Lockman Foundation. Used by permission.

This book is dedicated to each of our children,
Kimberli, Anna, Timothy, and Jonathan,
who continue to live the story. . . .

Contents

Acknowledgments

Special thanks . . .

—*To our friends at Focus on the Family,*
especially Mike Yorkey, to whom we'll always be indebted
for helping us put our vision in print.

—*To David and MaryLynne Hazard,*
for believing in the key talk concept enough
to pursue its publication.

—*To Paul Thigpen,*
whose godly character and faith
have permeated the pages of this book
as he labored with us in preparation of the manuscript.

Foreword

I like what I hear from Ric and Renée Durfield—and we need a whole lot more voices like theirs.

I watched Ric speak to over fifteen hundred Christian leaders gathered at our annual Pastors Conference at The Church On The Way. I studied the faces of teens, parents, and singles the night he spoke to nearly three thousand present at our church. It is clear that I'm not alone in liking these people.

The reason is easily explained: They have a handle on workable *reality*. They're more than a pair with convictions—they're people with a practical answer to a real problem, and they have a warm, genuine way of presenting it. *Raising Your Kids to Be Sexually Pure* communicates a tender truth in a convincing way. It's another kind of "tough love" that has been forged in the fire of this generation's hellish attacks on biblical morality.

You don't need to pastor an urban congregation in America's second largest city to know we're in the hellfire-level heat of a revolt against *all* moral values of proven worth. Like the second Psalm's description of the radical assault of mere men upon God's Messiah, our generation is throwing off every restraint. And the disastrous results are no longer imminent—they've arrived.

Amid this scene, the demise of sexual purity as a desirable trait has all but swept the entire teenage culture before it. Only the fear of suicide by promiscuity, by reason of the AIDS plague, has dulled the point of this phalanx-like thrust into a whole generation of youth.

But as grateful as anyone may be for anything that dissuades a young person from immorality, there are a lot better reasons for staying pure than simply keeping well. And it's here that the Durfields begin their own kind of confrontation with a mind-set—presenting us with a positive, assertive, practical "ways and means" handbook for leading youth in a *new revolution*.

I feel it's important to note that the Durfields are an African-American couple. I mention their race because it is doubly fulfilling for me to see Ric and Renée's rising influence. As pastor of an interracial congregation, I am especially concerned over the fact that generations of injustice have tended to reduce the black male to a stereotype. It may be the shoe-shine boy of a past generation or the Olympic athlete of the '90s—but in either case, the mind and the leadership of the man is too seldom seen or honored. Ric's model, and the way Renée so magnificently teams with him, provides a study all of us of every race can learn from—and show our families how to live the same way.

From the platform of the church they lead so fruitfully, to the cover of James Dobson's *Focus on the Family* magazine,

Ric's and Renée's faces keep "turning up." And everywhere they do, they are turning people on! Along with their kids, who dramatically prove the point Mom and Dad make in their lectures and seminars, the Durfields are evidence for a deep belief I hold—that God isn't through with this perverse generation. He's raising up people like these, through whom I believe He's intending to accomplish a societal turnaround.

I've watched Ric's life from the days he was in college, through the early years of his marriage and ministry, and right up and into these years of his appearance as an ascending voice to our nation's parents and teens. And the best thing I can say is this: He's real, he's steadfast, he's trustworthy.

There's a reason for that: He knows the Man who makes a man, a marriage, and a family. And as Ric stands tall in his life and ministry for Jesus Christ, he's helping others learn to rise beyond the tide of the times. This book provides a *handle*—a tool for gaining leverage to lift us from the moral quicksand sucking so many downward. And it provides a *hope*—a Rock for solid footing that will stand the test of all our tomorrows.

Jack W. Hayford, D. Litt.
Senior Pastor
The Church On The Way
Van Nuys, California

Introduction

Much has happened since 1991, when *Raising Them Chaste* was released. Published reports and journal articles based on the National Longitudinal Study of Adolescent Health, published in June 2001, are acknowledging the positive impact that virginity pledges have had on teenage sexual activity.

The virginity pledge movement began in April of 1990, when "A Promise With a Ring to It" was featured in *Focus on the Family* magazine. The article reveals how the virginity pledge had its beginnings. It was in 1978, when our oldest daughter, Kimberli, was eleven years old. Renée and I had an idea: to have a private, personal, and intimate time with the child to explain conception, the biblical view of marriage, and the sacredness of sexual purity. It was to be a time when a mom and daughter or a dad and son could candidly discuss the questions, fears, and anxieties of adolescence. We called it a "key talk."

We also had another idea. At the time of the key talk, the parent presents a specially made "key" ring to the son or daughter. The ring, which symbolizes a commitment with God, is worn by the adolescent during the difficult teen and young adult years.

Since that time, organizations around the world have adapted their own variations of this powerful concept. Scores of individual churches and entire denominations, such as the Southern Baptist Church, have used this concept to encourage millions of teens to commit to virginity pledges, in which they promise to abstain from sex until marriage.

We have always viewed the concept as a gift to the Body of Christ. It is our sincere desire that God will continue to use it to draw families together around the love of Jesus Christ and to preserve future generations that will glorify His name.

1

A Generation at Risk

Ron, a seventh grader whose family is close to ours, seemed to have everything going for him. He was a bright young man, raised in a Christian home, and happy to have a growing friendship with a pretty girl at his school.

One afternoon when he was home alone, Ron slit his wrists.

Why? As it turns out, some older boys at school—quite popular with the girls—had told him some weeks before that his girlfriend wanted to go to bed with him. He'd resisted the idea because his parents had taught him clearly that premarital sex was wrong. But the boys had continued to badger and challenge him, accusing him of not being "man enough" to do it.

One day after school Ron was particularly confused and upset by their taunts. As he walked home, he thought, "I'm a Christian and I can't have sex. Why should a failure like me even be alive? I should kill myself."

The depression deepened that afternoon, and though his parents noticed he was disturbed, they weren't sure how to help. They had to leave the house for a short while, and while they were gone, Ron sat down on the couch and slit his veins.

We thank God that Ron lived to tell the story. The blood that began to gush from his arms seemed to wake him out of a dream. He bandaged himself and called for help.

Today Ron is in the eleventh grade and still a virgin. He says soberly: "I know now how close I came to tragedy—either by having sex or by committing suicide—over the words of friends that really weren't friends at all."

The greater tragedy is that Ron is not alone. Grim statistics tell the story in disturbing black and white: Pressured or seduced into sexual sin by an increasingly immoral culture, millions of youth in our nation are suffering from the grave emotional and physical consequences of promiscuity. As a result, today's young generation is a *generation at risk*.

Many of us may have assumed that the AIDS scare would reduce the incidence of sexual activity among American youth. But research would seem to indicate only a positive, proactive approach is effective.

According to the National Survey of Family Growth, in 1982 only 19 percent of girls under the age of fifteen in this country were sexually experienced. By 1990 that number had increased to nearly 29 percent, and 70 percent of all American teenagers were having sex by age eighteen.

Since 1991, however, that trend has been changing. According to the Centers for Disease Control and Prevention (CDC), "during 1991–2001 the percentage of U.S. high school students who ever had sexual intercourse and the percentage who had multiple sex partners decreased" (*MMWR Weekly*, September 27, 2002/51 (38); 856–859).

Specifically, they reported that during this same period (1991–2001) "the prevalence of sexual experience decreased 16 percent among high school students" (Ibid.). Even the birth rate has been affected. According to statistics supplied by The National Center for Health, "the teen birth rate reached a record low in 2000, with rates steadily declining throughout the 1990s" (June 19, 2002).

In spite of these encouraging trends, the numbers still reflect a high incidence of sexual activity, with many accompanying social problems.

The Alan Guttmacher Institute reported in 2002 that "By their 18th birthday, 6 in 10 teenage women and nearly 7 in 10 teenage men have had sexual intercourse."[1] Nearly 25 percent of American infants are currently born to unmarried mothers. Teens make up 13 percent of the overall birth rate in the United States (according to the Alan Guttmacher Institute), and a whopping 70 percent of these unwed teen mothers go on welfare. Of those teens who marry because of getting pregnant, 60 percent will be divorced within five years.

Eighty-five percent of all American teens have had sex by age nineteen.[2]

Another sobering social consequence of our sexual revolution is the proliferation of sexually transmitted diseases. One in four sexually active teens, according to the Centers for Disease Control, will contract a venereal disease before they finish high school. As a matter of fact, the CDC also reports that "it is estimated that about half of all new HIV infections in the United States are among young people under the age of 25." They are currently contracting 2.5 million reported cases of STDs a year. Meanwhile, 20 to 30 percent of college-age women are estimated to have genital herpes, which sadly is incurable.

The AIDS epidemic in itself is enough to terrify parents with its potential disaster. We used to read the biblical book of Revelation and shudder at the thought of its prophecies about plagues that would wipe out large segments of the earth's population. We would think soberly, "We wouldn't want to be here when *that* is happening."

Now we realize, however, that a plague of that sort *is* here, and it's spreading. AIDS has the potential to wipe out whole nations. An estimated one million Americans are infected with the AIDS virus, and more than forty million are affected worldwide. The 'Morbidity and Mortality Weekly Report' (1996) shows the following trend. In 1981, when AIDS was first recognized in the United States, there were fewer than sixty reported cases. By 1994 more than forty thousand U.S. residents had died from AIDS. By 1996 AIDS had become the leading cause of death among persons 25 to 44 years of age.

This epidemic was created by the promiscuity of our generation in only a few short years, and we are now seeing the wages of our sin. Of course, many people have contracted AIDS through no fault of their own, including hundreds of infants who were infected by their mothers. Yet most of the spread of this dreaded disease has been through immoral sexual activity and drug use. John W. Santrock ("Life-Span Development" Sixth Edition) states that 1–1.5 million Americans are now asymptomatic carriers of AIDS. They are infected but show no signs or clinical symptoms. The Ninth Edition also states that in 2003 alone there were four thousand newly reported cases of AIDS in children 13 to 19 years old.

In the African-American and Hispanic communities, the figures about promiscuity and disease continue to tell an especially desperate story—but one that also has indications of hope. For example, even though births to teenagers in these communities continue to be substantially higher than for other groups in the U.S., the CDC's statistics show that their teen birth rate actually *declined* by 30 percent over the past decade to a historic low, and the rate for black teens in particular was down by more than 40 percent. For young black teens (ages 15 to 17), the results were even more striking—the rate has been cut *in half* since 1991. But we are still faced with the appalling fact that a full 70 percent of all black babies born in the U.S. are born to unwed mothers, with an infant mortality rate of nearly one in five.

Less obvious but just as damaging are the psychological and spiritual consequences of these statistics. Not long ago one of our daughters was having a frank talk with a young single male friend. She spoke boldly about her personal standards of sexual purity and how she was committed to being a virgin until marriage.

As she talked, her friend grew increasingly somber. At last he spoke frankly himself, with deep sadness in his voice.

"I wish I had long ago established the standards you did," he said to her. "You see, even though I've never been married, I've fathered fourteen children. But I've never seen any of them because they're all in heaven—most of them were aborted, and the others were miscarried."

That young man carries the burden of a multiple tragedy that will probably weigh on him to one degree or another for the rest of his life. And countless other young people are like him.

Those who engage in sex outside marriage and give birth to or abort babies are finding themselves saddled with a burden of guilt and low self-esteem. They're disillusioned with sex, relationships, and marriage. They feel used and confused, betrayed and marred. No doubt in cases like that of our daughter's young friend, the pressures of our society's sexual chaos have also contributed to the soaring teen suicide rate in this country.

Christian parents may assume that their children are somehow safe from the terrible results of these alarming statistics simply because of their faith and church environment. Yet some surveys suggest that many teens with a professed spiritual commitment differ little from their peers in sexual activity. Evidently, having Christian parents and being actively involved in church offers no guarantee that a teen is immune to the pressures pushing them into premarital sexual involvement. Today, in spite of some promising trends among high school students, young people of all backgrounds are having more sex, more babies, more abortions—and at an earlier age—than ever before.

Why the Trend?

What exactly are the pressures that are pushing our young people in this direction, and why are they failing to resist the push? Before we adults judge this younger generation too quickly, we do well to remember what it was like when we were their age—and then to realize that the pressures today are greater than ever before. In fact, we believe that the sexual challenges faced by earlier generations cannot even be compared in intensity to those faced by our young people today.

As it was for us, the onset of puberty brings with it a growing sexual awareness and desire. Hormones cause the same reactions today as they did a generation ago. But teens are facing additional problems that many of today's adults never encountered.

First, puberty is arriving sooner than ever before. Only forty years ago the average age for its onset was fourteen; today it's closer to twelve. That means those physical changes and feelings are taking place when kids are less emotionally mature, and young people have more years during which they must keep their sexual urges under control.

Second, children tend to mature faster intellectually these days than in times past, and they certainly have more access to information about sex, which can raise their curiosity. Yet despite rapid physical and intellectual growth, they seem to be maturing emotionally more slowly than their parents did—perhaps because of less contact with adults. Grown-ups in their extended families are absent; family schedules are busier than ever; latchkey kids spend most of their time with peers and the media; and more families than ever are headed by single parents.

Third, the waiting period till marriage has gotten longer on the other end as well, with many people delaying that commitment until their mid- to late twenties or early thirties. A hundred years ago, people typically had to wait a couple of years at most between the time of sexual awakening and marriage. But now an interlude of ten to twenty years is not uncommon.

Finally, our contemporary culture relentlessly preaches a message of sexual amorality, undermining the traditional conviction that sex should be reserved for marriage. Television, movies, magazines, and popular music today are reaching the saturation point with material that only a generation ago would have been labeled pornography, causing adolescents to daily hear countless seductive voices insisting that casual sex is normal and desirable, and that society has no firm moral standards by which to judge sexual behavior.

Equalizing the Pressure

In April 1963, the American nuclear submarine *Thresher* disappeared about two hundred miles off the coast of New England. Radio contact was lost as the vessel underwent deep submergence tests. The ensuing attempts to contact and then locate the *Thresher* were all in vain.

What happened? Apparently the submarine had traveled deeper than it was pressurized to go. The pressure of the waters on the outside simply exceeded the cabin pressure on the inside, and the vessel's walls collapsed. As a result, 129 sailors were lost.

> **We can plant within our sons and daughters a vision of sexual wholeness and purity that will strengthen their resolve to live with integrity—to say no to the world and be happy about saying it.**

Our children—and we ourselves, for that matter—are like that submarine. The external pressures against self-control never let up, and in fact they increase as our culture descends deeper and deeper into immorality. If the internal pressure is unequal to the external—if there's not something strong enough inside them that says no to temptation—then our young people too will collapse. The combined weight of hormones, media messages, and peer pressure will simply overwhelm them.

Sadly enough, many Christian parents today who want to help their kids in this regard feel paralyzed, unable to counsel and inspire their children to live holy lives. They have found that trying merely to erect a "fence" of rules and regulations around our youth won't work in the long run; there are too many opportunities for kids to jump the fence.

Our only hope, with the help of the Holy Spirit, is to equalize the pressure. We have to support our young people in building within themselves an ideal, an inner standard, that will exert sufficient counterpressure against the world. We can plant within our sons and daughters a vision of sexual wholeness and purity that will strengthen their resolve to live with integrity—to say *no* to the world and be happy about saying it.

We read in the book of Daniel the thrilling story about how three young Hebrew people—Shadrach, Meshach, and Abednego—risked their lives to stand firm for what they believed, despite the behavior of their peers. When King Nebuchadnezzar commanded them to worship an idol on pain of death, they refused for the sake of righteousness, even when everyone else in the nation obeyed the command. And they explained their stance calmly but forcefully to the king and all who were within hearing distance (Daniel 3).

We believe God wants those three young men to serve as a model for all young Christians in taking a stand for righteousness. We believe He wants our children to be able to look their peers in the eye and say, "I'm a virgin. I'm thankful to God that I am. And I wish you were too." We believe He wants them to stop being defensive about their standards and go on the offensive toward the false standards of the world.

Kids Long for Our Direction

One day soon after our oldest son, Tim, began college, a group of students gathered around him to challenge his claim that he was still a virgin. They pointed out how he had an active social life and that there was no way he could have remained sexually pure while dating so many pretty girls. But by the time Tim had explained to them who he was in Christ and how that motivated him to maintain his standards, they were convinced he was telling the truth, and it made a lasting impression on them.

How do children get to the place where they can take that kind of public stand for righteousness among their peers? There are no easy or quick answers to that question, no formulas guaranteed to make our kids into models of virtue. Yet amid so much bad news about our young people, the good news is that parents do in fact play a major role in their teens' moral development and that God has placed them in the best position to help kids grow into godly maturity. Despite all the ups and downs of learning to live under the same roof, and all the unholy influences of the world, children nevertheless grow up looking at their parents as primary models and authorities.

Negative peer pressure and media messages no doubt take their toll on children's respect for their parents. Yet in 1983 the Search Institute, conducting a study of families who attended church, discovered that adolescents showed an overwhelming preference for their parents as the people they would most like to turn to for help and advice with questions about sex. This was especially the case for younger adolescents, but even a majority of high school freshmen preferred their parents' counsel and encouragement to that of friends or other adults.

As Christian parents, then, we have not only a God-given responsibility, but also a precious opportunity to help our kids cultivate moral stamina to withstand the world's pressures. Though they may not always show it, they *long* for us to give them moral direction, to set an example for them, and to answer their questions.

Our children are like the tender young shoots in a vegetable garden described by author David C. Needham:

> Every year I plant a row of pole string beans in our backyard. Soon after a seed sprouts in the damp spring soil, its tendril begins to reach upward. Moving back and forth. Searching. Groping for something that will direct its climb. Eventually, if it finds nothing, it will collapse to the dirt. Continuing to twist and turn it will often grab hold of itself in a desperate attempt to find some support for climbing. Ultimately, it will become a tangled confusion with a pittance of the harvest it might have had.
>
> But if it finds a pole . . . it will become artistry in motion. Climbing higher and higher. Lush foliage, blossoms. And long, crisp string beans.
>
> David C. Needham, *The Birthright*,
> Multnomah, 1979, p. 171

Our children *need* our support and direction if they're to flourish and be fruitful, contrary to modern philosophies that teach young people to be highly independent.

Children are so anxious to have adult guidance that we actually have non-Christian kids from other families coming to us to ask our help in remaining sexually pure. The certainty and security of a standard appeals to them, because they're sick of being pushed around and they want to stand for something they believe in. So when we present them with a clear and firm standard, in the light of the reasons such a standard is worthy of their commitment, we're finding that they are more than willing to take hold of it and make it their own.

Obviously, God has given our young people the same free will He has given us. We can't manipulate them into compliance to a standard, nor can we make their choices for them.

But we can clarify the choices, model the right choices, and demonstrate the rewards of those right choices.

No one says it's easy. We have to learn whole new dimensions of prayer and reliance on the Holy Spirit, and we will likely make some wrong choices ourselves as we try to guide and inspire our children. But we can take courage in knowing that God desires our children's sexual purity even more than we do, and that His Holy Spirit will be our Counselor as we try to be theirs. The promise Solomon made to his child is the same promise our Father makes to us:

> If you call out for insight and cry aloud for understanding, and if you look for it as for silver and search for it as for hidden treasure, then you will understand the fear of the Lord and find the knowledge of God. For the Lord gives wisdom, and from his mouth come knowledge and understanding.
>
> Proverbs 2:3–6 NIV

The "Key Talk" Concept

In our experience as parents of four adult children, we've found that the Lord does indeed give wisdom to those who seek Him for it. We've had our difficult times as all parents have, yet God has proven His faithfulness again and again.

As we sought over the years to help our children cultivate and live by an inner standard of righteousness, especially with regard to sexual purity, we asked the Holy Spirit to give us a divine creativity. One of His answers to our prayer came some years ago, when our children were young, as we were reading the bestseller by Dr. James Dobson, *Dare to*

Discipline. In that insightful book he told of a plan he had in mind for his daughter, who at the time was five years old:

> I hope to give my daughter a small gold key on her tenth birthday. It will be attached to a chain to be worn around her neck and will represent the key to her heart. Perhaps she will give that key to one màn only, the one who will share her love through the remainder of her life.

> James Dobson, *Dare to Discipline*, Tyndale, 1970

That simple idea struck us as a good one to practice ourselves. But before long the "gold key" had developed into a larger parenting strategy, which we came to call a "key talk." This book is about that particular strategy.

One of the great hurdles for parents who need and want to talk with their teens about sexual integrity is that they often feel awkward doing so. They're not sure about the appropriate time and place for such a conversation; they may lack confidence in their own ability to answer questions or establish boundaries; and they worry that their teen's response may be less than enthusiastic. For some parents, the situation may even be complicated by a sense of guilt lingering from their own moral failures when they were young; they don't want to be hypocrites, and they wonder whether, in light of their own experience, a firm standard of sexual purity is simply unrealistic.

We hope that this book, and the key talk strategy it describes, will provide a practical approach to meet the need of these families. Of course, we must recognize at the outset that we're not trying to offer the key talk as some quick fix to a complicated problem. We're convinced that a total approach to this challenge requires a long-term quality relationship between parent and child that includes, but is not limited to, praying with the child, playing with the child, and participating in activities that might be of interest to the child. We want to include in this book some suggestions for cultivating that kind of relationship.

Nevertheless, we've found that the key talk can make a significant contribution toward forging a parent-child friendship that becomes a vessel of God's grace, characterized by openness, honesty, and mutual respect. We've tried it with each of our children, learning more each time about how to make it effective. Meanwhile, other parents have joined us in taking this simple, practical approach to strengthening their children's inner standards—so many that we now direct a ministry called *For Wedlock Only*, whose purpose is to help families in this critical area. We're grateful to God to be able to say that the key talk strategy has helped not just our children, but many others as well to stand strong in their decision to remain pure in a world that often despises virginity.

In the following chapters we'll present a practical plan for the key talk—how to prepare for it, how to hold it successfully, and how to follow up on it for maximum effectiveness. We'll also suggest some ideas for praying for your kids, answering their questions, keeping open the lines of communication, and providing dating guidelines that will support rather than undermine their commitment to purity.

In addition, we'll let our children say for themselves what the key talk has meant to them. We'll discuss some special hurdles you may encounter as you work and pray with your children through their own challenges. Finally, we'll suggest some ways in which the key talk concept could be used in situations beyond the teen years: with older single children, divorced people, unmarried parents, and others who might desire "surrogate" parents to support them in remaining sexually pure.

If parents are to meet the challenge of helping their children stay sexually pure, they need a constant reliance on the Holy Spirit through prayer and a practical strategy for approaching the matter. To share with you how the key talk can be an important part of their approach, we first need to tell you how we have used it in our own family.

Points to Remember

- Statistics show the alarming incidence of sexual promiscuity in our society and its devastating consequences. On the whole, churched kids show the same trends as unchurched kids.

- Our young people face unprecedented pressures to be sexually active: earlier puberty, a longer wait till marriage, less supportive contact with adults, and relentless media messages that sex outside marriage is the norm.

- Parents are in a better position than anyone else to help children cultivate an internal counterpressure to resist sexual temptation.

- The key talk concept has been proven effective in many families as a strategy for encouraging children to remain sexually pure.

1. The Alan Guttmacher Institute (AGI), *In Their Own Right: Addressing the Sexual and Reproductive Health Needs of American Men*, New York, AGI, 2002.

2. The 1995 National Survey of Family Growth (NSFG). Published by U.S. Dept. of Health & Human Services' Centers for Disease Control & Prevention.

2

What Is a Key Talk?

With a flourish, the hostess seated Richard and our youngest child, Jonathan, in the main dining room of a nice restaurant near our home. The fancy furnishings, subdued lighting, and pricey menu told our fifteen-year-old that this night was to be a special occasion.

As they scanned the large red menus, Richard mentally reviewed what he wanted to say to Jonathan. Our son knew they had gone out for his key talk, a time specially set aside for a discussion of any questions he might have about sexuality.

Of course, Jonathan already knew the basics of sex education. We had raised him in a home with the express family policy that "no question is dumb." He had begun learning from us about the human body in his preschool days, and from then up through the ninth-grade health class on human reproduction he had recently completed, Jonathan had had ample opportunity to ask questions about the topic.

Nevertheless, this night the conversation would go far beyond human anatomy and physiology to include the special meaning of commitment and honor for a young man who was fast growing up. When the chilled jumbo shrimp appetizers arrived at the table, Richard leaned over quietly toward Jonathan.

"Tonight is your night, son," Richard began. "This is a special time for you and Dad to talk about any sexual questions that might still be on your mind. If you've ever had questions that might have seemed a little awkward, well, tonight is the right time to ask them. Nothing is off limits tonight.

"If anything's been bothering you about your body or adolescence or marriage or whatever, it's okay to talk about it now. As we work our way through the meal this evening, I want you just to be thinking about any questions you might have."

At that time in his development, we knew, Jonathan was much more interested in riding his mountain bike through the hills near our home in LaVerne, California, than chasing after girls. But he was maturing rapidly, so we also knew this talk was coming none too soon. When he first sat down, Jonathan had seemed a little uncomfortable as he looked nervously around. But as he and his dad began talking, he relaxed a bit.

Our son, who at that time had never been on a date, wanted to know first *for sure* what "the line" was. How far was *too* far? He thought he had a good idea of the boundaries, but he wanted to hear it from his father.

"A light kiss is about as far as you can go," Richard replied. "Sexual emotions are very strong, and if you're not careful, you'll do things you don't want to do. So you need to avoid anything that leads you up to that."

They discussed the matter then in more detail—such as what kinds of kissing were off limits. Richard noted, for example, that kissing a girl on the neck can lead to going much farther. The conversation continued until Richard had answered to Jonathan's satisfaction all the questions he'd been pondering for a while.

The Ring and the Covenant

As the main dishes were being cleared away, Richard told Jonathan that it was time to make a commitment before the Lord. Of course, that restaurant table was not the most private place available, but we felt that a more public setting added to the significance of what our son was about to do.

Jonathan was to pray, making a covenant with God, but first Richard had to provide a context for what he was doing. They talked about the seriousness of a covenant commitment and reviewed all the reasons why sexual purity was a standard Jonathan needed to make his own. Then it was time to pray together.

"Son," Richard said, "this covenant will be something between you and God until you're married. We're going to include your future wife in this prayer. We'll ask God that whoever she is and wherever she is, He'll be with her as well. We'll ask Him to help her to be pure until the time you're married.

> Our son . . . wanted to know for sure what "the line" was. How far was too far? . . . He thought he knew, but he wanted to hear it from his father.

"Then I want you to ask God for His grace to keep this covenant, because even though you may have right inten-

35

tions, sometimes things go wrong. I want you to pray, and then Dad will pray."

Jonathan turned to his father and took his hands. It surprised Richard a little that his son would be so bold in a public restaurant, yet he realized that this was precisely the kind of boldness Jonathan would need in order to stand alone when necessary to keep his covenant with God.

Jonathan bowed his head and prayed fervently. Then it was Richard's turn. Before he prayed, he said, "Jonathan, I have something for you." He took out a custom-made fourteen-carat gold ring, engraved with a key symbol, and slipped it onto our son's finger as a token of the covenant he was making. Bowing their heads, Richard then asked the Lord to honor that covenant and help Jonathan to resist temptation in the coming years.

As Jonathan and his dad left the restaurant that night, a couple sitting at a nearby booth stopped them. They said that they couldn't help but notice that something special had happened. They were right: Something special *had* happened, and it was between Jonathan, his wife-to-be— whoever, wherever she was—and the Lord.

The Beginnings of the Key Talk

Jonathan was the fourth and last of our children to have a key talk. By that time we had learned a great deal from getting so much practice! As we mentioned in the last chapter, the whole idea had started ten years before when we read Dr. Dobson's idea about giving his daughter a key to wear, and we decided to try it ourselves. At that time we had taken the "key" thought and expanded it for our oldest child, Kimberli, who was then a mature eleven-year-old and fully developed physically.

First of all, though we liked Dr. Dobson's idea of presenting his daughter a key to wear around her neck, we decided to give Kimberli a custom-made "key ring," which in her case was actually a key wrapped around into a ring shape. Our reason for that choice was that a ring is used in wedding ceremonies as a sign of commitment.

From a practical standpoint as well, we speculated that in gym class or other active settings, a necklace chain could easily be broken and the key lost, while a ring might remain in place more securely. We must admit, however, that our son Jonathan took off the valued ring while playing sports and lost it, and we had to replace it. For that reason, we encourage parents to emphasize to their children that the ring shouldn't come off. If necessary, they can always have it re-polished or have a stone replaced.

Why did we have our daughter's ring made from a key? The purpose of a key is to unlock a door, and we wanted the ring to symbolize the key to our daughter's heart and her virginity. It would also represent a covenant between Kimberli and God in which she would promise to keep herself pure for her future husband, and God would respond with grace to help her.

As she wore it daily, the key ring would serve throughout the difficult teen and young adult years as a powerful and strengthening reminder of the value and beauty of virginity and of the importance of reserving sex for marriage. It would also encourage her that God would honor her commitment and bless her faithfulness. And on her wedding night—that sacred evening when a life of sexual experience could begin in its proper setting—she could take the ring off and present it to her new husband as a precious gift, telling him all that it represents.

In addition, however, we realized that our daughter

needed a special time to talk about what the ring symbolized and to verbalize her commitment to God in prayer. We thought that at the same time we should make sure we had answered her remaining questions about sexuality. And we wanted to do all this in a memorable setting that would set it off as a once-in-a-lifetime event to be remembered.

The result: Renée arranged to take Kimberli out to dinner at a fancy Mexican restaurant for the key talk. At the time we were laboring to build a young and struggling congregation, so finances were tight, and a dinner out was an added expense. But our willingness to save up the money for that evening was in itself an indication to our daughter how much we valued the time she and her mother would have together.

Because dressing up is one way people recognize the significance of an extraordinarily special occasion, such as a wedding or a graduation ceremony, Renée insisted that the two of them put on their best for the evening. Jeans and sweatshirts just wouldn't have conveyed the sense of importance that particular event deserved.

Kimberli was a bit anxious, but Renée's encouraging attitude soon put her at ease. She asked questions and Renée replied, even drawing anatomical diagrams on the paper napkins when necessary! Kimberli knew most of the basics about human sexuality, such as where babies came from. But this was a time to talk about how the act of sex was to be an act of love between husband and wife.

Renée was still a young mother, and this was her first child. No one had ever had such a talk with Renée herself when she was young. So there were a few times that night when she had to overcome some slight feelings of embarrassment—usually when Kimberli asked an unexpected question. But Renée nevertheless answered each question as simply and directly as she could, and Kimberli was satisfied.

The conversation's atmosphere was full of excitement and warmth, and it made a deep and lasting impression on our daughter. Renée recalls her own priority that night of affirming the essential goodness and naturalness of sex within the bonds of marriage. Evidently, she was successful in that regard. Today Kimberli says, "I especially remember my mother telling me that sex was not our idea, but God's, so it had to be good."

After the talk, Renée pulled out the silver ring we had had specially made for the occasion. She said, "Honey, now you're going to get a special gift, coming from my heart, Dad's heart, and the Lord's heart." The gift totally surprised and pleased her as she responded with squeals of delight.

After talking together about the commitment Kimberli was making, mother and daughter joined hands to talk to God. Then they agreed in prayer that our daughter would have the strength to remain sexually pure. Though the full understanding of a covenant was not at that time as well-developed in our key talk as it was later with Jonathan, still the importance of Kimberli's commitment was clear.

From that day on, our daughter began showing her ring to her friends and telling them what it meant. Today, as a successful adult, Kimberli reflects: "That ring was a constant reminder—and got me through some tough times! I'm now considering marriage, and I look forward to the day when my husband will receive my key ring as a token of the pledge I made to the Lord."

Different Timing for Different Young People

A few years later it was time to have the key talk with Anna, our second child. Kimberli, knowing the importance of the evening, kept the specific contents of the key talk a secret from her younger sister. But Anna knew something wonderful had happened the night Renée and Kimberli had gone out, and she was full of excitement that now it was to be her turn. She and her mom talked about it and planned it for months.

Looking back, Anna realizes that the night of the key talk forged a new bond between her mother and herself. She says, "It's impossible to say how important our conversation was in my life."

Anna's ring was different from her sister's. Renée searched for weeks and finally found a beautiful silver ring (gold was more than we could afford at the time) with a Holy Spirit dove on it. We had a little zirconium stone set into the ring and had a key engraved on it as well.

Anna's course of development was also different from her sister's. She was not interested in boys until a later age; at fourteen she was still playing with dolls and going to bed with teddy bears. In addition, puberty came later for her than it had for her sister. So we determined that her key talk should not come as early as Kimberli's had.

When Renée opened the conversation, Anna was surprised at how easily she could speak with her mother about sexuality without feeling any sense of guilt. Renée seemed to understand well what Anna was feeling and thinking.

Looking back, Anna realizes that the night of the key talk forged a new bond between her mother and herself. She says, "It's impossible to say how important that conversation was in my life."

Today Anna remembers: "I had strong sexual feelings; I had a Christian boyfriend for nearly four years, and we spent precious moments together. But because I made a stand from Day One of our relationship not to have sex, I was able to keep the covenant with God that I made the night of our key talk."

The key talk with our third child, Timothy, was the first one for Richard to have. So he was a bit nervous about how to approach it. Yet Tim's own enthusiasm about the event encouraged him.

Tim had been a late bloomer like Anna. He had simply not been interested in girls as early as his brother—Jonathan had begun asking questions about them at the age of six! But by the time we had our key talk, Tim was quite ready for the occasion.

As it turned out, Richard and Tim enjoyed the evening so much that they felt as if they were the only two people in the restaurant as they relaxed over the meal. Knowing that this particular night was an "appointed" time to discuss sexuality made it easier for them to do it without intimidation. Richard was proud to be alone with his oldest son addressing a subject that was so critical to his success; Tim was just as proud to be with his dad because he knew he really cared.

The high point of that evening came when Tim offered his prayer of commitment to God. As he and Richard held hands and bowed their heads, Richard began to weep. He heard Tim utter words to the Lord reflecting a depth he'd never known Tim had. It sounded as if an angel had slipped in between them to say the words because they reflected a wisdom and eloquence usually far beyond a teenager's years.

Tim recalls: "I remember anticipating the day I would make a long-term commitment to God. I felt I was doing something that would make God happy with me. God has always been someone I've wanted to please, and I know if I keep this covenant with Him and don't break it, God will smile upon me.

"I've kept that commitment. I've only dated girls who have the same morals as I do. I'm still tempted, but that ring on my finger reminds me of my covenant with God and the gift I'll someday give to my wife—a gift I've never given anybody else."

Other Families Try It Out

When we introduced the key talk to our family, we never dreamed that it would someday lead to our establishing a ministry to share the strategy with other families. We simply developed the approach because we believed it would help give our kids the courage to stand up to their peers and against secular society. We wanted to strengthen them in their resolve to set the kind of standards other young people would follow, to take the offensive instead of feeling on the defensive.

Nevertheless, in time other families heard about the key talk and began asking how they could have one as well. The requests for help became so great that we established For Wedlock Only, a ministry dedicated to supporting families in this area. (For materials available through this ministry, see the contact information in the back of the book.)

When Dr. Dobson invited us to discuss our idea on one of his radio broadcasts, we were thrilled to share what we had learned. But we were quite unprepared for the response: Over fifty thousand people called and wrote in the following months, asking for help in setting up key talks in their families.

In light of that overwhelming expression of need, we decided that these parents needed a more detailed presentation of our strategy. So the next few chapters will describe how *you* can have a key talk with your own children—or with any children who want your help in establishing a covenant with God to remain sexually pure.

As you begin preparation for the key talk, we should note that if at all possible, a mother should have the talk with a daughter and a father with a son. This will help avoid unnecessary embarrassment from having to discuss sensitive topics in human biology, sexuality, or romance with an adult of the opposite sex. It also allows for closer identification when the parent answers questions or makes points by using illustrations from his or her own experience.

At the same time, however, we want to assure single parents that they can still have this talk effectively with a child of either sex. God gives us the grace for whatever situation we may find ourselves in.

Points to Remember

- The key talk developed in our family as a way of providing our children with an adequate sexual education and supporting them in making a commitment to God to remain sexually pure.
- We discovered that the appropriate age to have the key talk varies according to the individual child, and different children will have different concerns to raise.

3

The Power of Covenant

Each year, three million photos are taken of the Rose Parade and Rose Bowl in Pasadena, California, making the tournament the most photographed event in the world. Amazingly enough, even though the game takes place in the midst of California's rainy season, camera buffs can almost always count on sunshine for their pictures. In a hundred years, it has rained only nine times during the Rose Parade.

How do you explain that remarkable statistic? Some Christians in the Pasadena area believe it has to do with a little-known detail of the event's early history. A century ago, the organizers of the Rose Parade made a commitment never to hold it on Sunday because they didn't want the celebration to compete in any way with worship services. They insisted that if New Year's Day—the normally scheduled date—fell on "the Sabbath," as they called it, then the parade would be held instead on Monday.

Since that time, American culture has largely abandoned the notion that Sunday should be set aside as a day to glorify God. In fact, over the years, professional sports and television have combined to make watching football games on Sunday something of an American tradition. Yet the Tournament of Roses Association still maintains the "never on Sunday" policy. In response, some Christians in Southern California maintain that God has blessed the commitment to honor Him by gracing the event with many years of beautiful weather.

Is there truly a connection between the parade policy and the weather? Only God Himself could say for sure. Nevertheless, like a parable, the story illustrates one of the central dynamics of a covenant commitment to God: When we commit ourselves to honoring Him, He responds with the grace we need to keep our commitment.

The "Key Talk" Covenant

This kind of covenant with God lies at the heart of the key talk strategy. A young person's promise to remain sexually pure is not like some long-term New Year's resolution in which the child simply resolves to act a certain way. Nor is it a mere agreement with the parent to obey a rule. It's a covenant made by a young person to honor God with his or her mind, heart, and body in the firm confidence that He will provide the grace to keep the commitment.

As temptations come, we don't want our children relying only on their own willpower to keep a resolution. When our kids are away from us, we don't want them simply adhering to a standard of behavior because Mom and Dad said to do it. In the long run that won't provide them with enough strength to resist the devil and stand strong.

Instead, we want God to go with them and give them the grace to honor Him with their sexuality. So rather than simply laying down rules or extracting resolutions, we decided in our family to bring our kids into a covenant with the Lord regarding sexual purity. That way the power of His acknowledged presence in their lives would help them to keep the covenant. When they are in a tight place, they know without a doubt that God is there to deliver them, to "provide the way of escape" from temptation (1 Cor. 10:13).

To prepare for leading your child into the key ring covenant, you may first need to spend some time studying what the Scriptures have to say about the nature of a covenant. Then, on the night of the key talk, you can share with your child from God's Word what it means to make a commitment to Him and why it is such a valuable step to take.

We realize that to some parents, this notion of a covenant may at first sound like an old-fashioned idea, hardly relevant to twenty-first century America. But as you discover what the Bible has to say about this special kind of commitment, we believe you'll become convinced that God Himself wants to give your child the power to live righteously. Knowing what the Scriptures say about the covenant should convince you that God Himself wants to support your child in his or her commitment to stay sexually pure.

The Biblical Meaning of "Covenant"

The biblical words we translate as "covenant" have their roots in the ancient practice of making a solemn commitment with a spoken promise and then sealing it with some kind of symbolic act and token. In its most general sense, an ancient covenant was a contract, an agreement, or a treaty between two parties.

For example, after a dispute over the fairness of their previous working relations, Laban and Jacob made a private covenant not to further defraud each other. They sealed it with an oath, a covenant meal, and a heap of stones gathered as a memorial to the agreement (Gen. 31:36–53). On an international level, King Asa of Judah and Ben-Hadad of Syria made a covenant to form a military alliance. It was sealed with a token of gold and silver gifts (1 Kings 15:19).

> **Because of the grace of the new covenant . . . this is not a contract in which God lays down a law . . . it's a loving promise from God that, by the Holy Spirit, He will . . . live through us so that we can obey Him.**

These kinds of covenants were rather common occurrences in both private and public life. But in the course of God's redemptive dealings with the world—first through the nation of Israel and then through His Son, Jesus Christ—the notion of a covenant was transformed into something much more significant. The great covenants of the Bible between God and His people are not contracts between two parties hammering out an agreement. Rather, they are promises made by God in which He graciously commits Himself to bless and care for the children He loves. Then, trusting in the grace He offers through His promises, His children are able to respond to God's initiative with a commitment of their own.

After the great Flood, for example, God established a covenant with Noah and his descendants that "never again will all life be cut off by the waters of a flood" (Gen. 9:11

NIV). Considering the terror Noah and his family had just suffered, they needed such an assurance in order to begin the process of rebuilding, with faith that their efforts would not be swept away by another catastrophe. So God graciously promised them His mercy and then sealed His promise with a token—the rainbow (v. 12).

Again, generations later when the Lord spoke to Abraham, He established a covenant with him, promising to make a great nation of his descendants and to give them a homeland (Gen. 12:1–3; 13:14–17; 15:1–18). God's promise allowed Abraham to trust in God's care and obey Him in faith. The covenant was sealed with the token of circumcision (Gen. 17:1–10).

Of course, the most important covenant of the Bible is the one Jesus made with His followers at the Last Supper: the "new covenant" of God's salvation enacted by Jesus' death and resurrection (Matt. 26:27–28). For Christians, this is the covenant with God that makes all other covenants possible. In it, God promises to forgive our sin and allow us to walk in fellowship with Him. He seals the promise with the gift of the indwelling Holy Spirit, whose power working through us makes it possible to live transformed lives that please Him (Eph. 1:14).

Because of the grace of the new covenant, which actually unites us to Him personally, we are free to respond to God with our own commitment to love and obey Him. This is not some contract in which God lays down a law and then blesses us if we keep it and curses us if we don't. Rather, it's a loving promise from God that by the Holy Spirit He will be with us, He will reveal Himself to us, and He will live through us so that we *can* obey Him (John 14:21, 23).

Obedience Becomes Possible

When God made it possible for the Jewish exiles to return home and rebuild Jerusalem, the people were deeply grateful for the mercy and power He had displayed on their behalf. The Lord had made a covenant with Abraham to give his descendants that land; and even though they had rebelled against God, He had kept His promise once more by reestablishing them in Judah.

Out of a heart of gratitude for this, the most recent blessing in a long history of divine blessings, the people came together in Jerusalem under Nehemiah's leadership and made a covenant with God. In response to all He had done for them, they publicly committed themselves to loving Him, honoring Him, and obeying His will (Nehemiah 9).

This event illustrates the kind of covenant we should make with God in response to the covenant He has made with us in Christ. In light of His great mercy that has redeemed us and given us new life in Jesus, we can commit ourselves in gratitude to walking in holiness with Him. Thus, our covenant with God is not a rule or a resolution, but rather the willing promise of a grateful heart.

The implications of these biblical truths for the key ring covenant are clear. First, we must help our children see that their sexuality is a good gift from God for which they can be thankful. (This insight can be emphasized in the key talk as you answer specific questions about sexual matters.) Then, we can point out how the best response of gratitude for God's kindness is a willing dedication of their sexuality to Him, a promise to honor Him by keeping that gift pure.

If our children have given their hearts to Jesus (and this is a good time to clarify that issue if it hasn't been before), they have already entered into His covenant of grace so that

Jesus lives within them. For that reason we need to share with them the further insight that if they are willing to respond gratefully with obedience to God's will—making their own covenant with God to keep themselves sexually pure—they can count on God to help them keep it.

This reality is a critical one to convey to our children. They need to know that when they make a covenant with God, He won't act like some cosmic "scorekeeper" standing over them to tally their failures. Instead, He'll be right alongside them when they're tempted, giving them the strength to resist and filling them with joy in their victories.

The covenant will inevitably be tested. Temptations will certainly come, and the battle to remain pure will sometimes be fierce. But God gives greater strength and grace when the temptation is severe, and such trying circumstances can serve to prove our allegiance to Him.

Even when they fail, our children can count on God's mercy and restoration. In the Old Testament, God told the prophet Hosea that His love for the immoral nation of Israel was like the persistent love of a man who cherishes his wife even though she has committed adultery (Hosea 2:13–20; 3:1–5). Such is the unfailing love of God for us today as well.

In the New Testament we find that the blood of Jesus not only secures our place in His covenant with us, it also secures our forgiveness when we fall short. The Bible tells us that "if we confess our sins, he is faithful and just and will forgive us our sins and purify us from all unrighteousness" (1 John 1:9 NIV.)

No doubt our children need to be aware that breaking a covenant is a serious matter with grave consequences. But they also need to know that to break a covenant is more than simply falling or failing to meet its conditions. Instead, breaking a covenant means to annul it by a persistent desire to live a lifestyle that is contrary to all that God promises. We may fall, but if we confess our sin to God and repent, we haven't broken the covenant. He will forgive us and restore us in covenant grace.

The Marriage Covenant

The covenant grace of salvation in Christ not only makes it possible to keep our commitments to God, it also gives us the grace to keep our covenants with one another.

The most important of those covenants with other people is the marriage commitment, a choice with far-reaching, lifelong consequences. In fact, our marriage vows are so important to God that He considers Himself a party in the covenant. When we pledge faithfulness to a spouse, we do it with Him as our witness, and we are accountable to Him for keeping it.

We see this reality clearly in the words of the prophet Malachi. When the men of ancient Judah divorced their wives, treating their marriage vows casually, the Lord rebuked them:

> Have we not all one Father? Did not one God create us? Why do we profane the covenant of our fathers by breaking faith with one another? . . . The Lord is acting as the witness between you and the wife of your youth, because you have broken faith with her, though she is your partner, the wife of your marriage covenant.
>
> Malachi 2:10, 14 NIV

In a sense, the key ring covenant can serve in our children's lives as a foreshadowing and even a precursor of the marriage covenant. Just because they can't yet ratify the marriage covenant with their future spouse doesn't mean they can't enter even now into the spirit of that covenant. On their wedding day, they will vow to "forsake all others." That vow will mean infinitely more if they can go into the marriage having from the beginning already "forsaken all others" with regard to giving themselves sexually.

That's one reason why we chose a ring as the token that seals the key ring covenant. The ring is an ancient symbol of the marriage vow, of faithfulness to one particular person for life. When our children make a covenant with God to remain sexually pure, the ring serves as a reminder that their future is in God's hands, and if He has marriage in mind for them, He will provide the right mate. It is important to emphasize that their covenant is first and foremost to remain faithful and obedient to God, and secondly to remain sexually pure for the partner whom God may have in store for them.

Covenant As a Way of Life

Much of the shaping of our children's attitudes and behavior in their early years is discipline-focused. But by the time they become teens, we should be giving primary attention to what might be called "life training"—the cultivation of wisdom by sharing insights and experiences that deal with the larger and deeper issues of life.

In that light, we should note that the key talk, with its emphasis on covenant commitment, can become the basis for sharing wisdom even in areas of life beyond sexuality. After all, in a sense, life is a series of commitments we make—to God, to ourselves, to our family and friends, to our employers and co-workers, to our community as a whole. To be a man or woman of integrity is to be a commitment-keeper.

For example, accepting a job can be seen as a commitment made with an employer to accomplish work assignments competently and reliably. Joining a church is a commitment made with a spiritual family to take part in the life of the congregation. Even an athlete's determination to train for a season in order to accomplish particular physical goals in cooperation with a team might be considered a commitment they make with themselves, the team, and their coaches.

The key talk can thus be a springboard for a number of future discussions that explore the meaning of critical character qualities. Using the idea of covenant as a foundational principle, you can talk with your child about the meaning of honesty and integrity, loyalty and faithfulness, persistence and dependability. Remember: What we leave *in* our children is more important than what we leave *to* them.

With all these insights in mind, you should be well prepared for your key talk discussion of covenant commitment. To keep the evening relaxed and informal, we encourage you to have a mental outline ready for the points you want to cover rather than bringing along a Bible (or this book) to the talk. Your child needs to know that the talk is coming from your heart. If you read the key talk material from a book, the evening might feel more like a formal lecture. Perhaps some of the key Scriptures you want your child to remember could be written out on a card for your child to study later and keep handy in his or her own Bible.

The other principal discussion in your key talk will involve explaining any matters about sexuality, romance, or dating that your child may be confused or curious about. So a second part of your preparation for the key talk is to anticipate the questions your child might have so that you'll be in the best possible position to answer them clearly and without embarrassment. For that reason, we turn next to a review of the questions that we have found teens in a key talk are most likely to ask.

Points to Remember

- To prepare for the key talk, you need to understand the biblical concept of a covenant so you can provide your child the proper context for making his or her promise to God.

- When God makes a covenant with us, He graciously commits Himself to love and care for us, and He calls us to respond with our own commitment to obey Him.

- The kind of covenant your child will make is not a contract in which God lays down the law and then enforces it with a threat to curse the one who breaks it. God promises to be with your child and live through him or her so your child can obey Him.

- The key covenant is not just a commitment to God; it's a foreshadowing and precursor of the marriage covenant your child may someday make.

- The key covenant can be a springboard for your child's growth in appreciating the importance of integrity, faithfulness, patience, and self-control in every area of life.

4

Questions Your Child May Ask

Renée still smiles over one particularly innocent but amusing question one of our children asked about sexual intercourse not long after the key talk.

"Mom," said the innocent young voice, "does it last all night?"

That question is typical of the kind of unexpected inquiry a key talk is bound to produce. Some matters we had never even thought to discuss will seem critical to our kids, and others that we thought for sure they would ask may not even come up. A few of their questions may even send us searching through reference works for the answer.

In a key talk we should simply expect the unexpected, keeping in mind that we haven't failed our child if we have to say, "I don't know the answer to that; let's find out together." But if we prepare for our children's questions ahead of time, thinking through the most commonly asked ones, we can at least keep the surprises to a minimum.

Perhaps the simplest way to approach the matter is to tell your child several weeks before the key talk the kinds of questions he or she will have the opportunity to ask. Suggest some topics of discussion like the following:

Bodily changes experienced in adolescence

Sexual intercourse

The reproductive process

Sexually transmitted diseases (STDs)

Masturbation

Dating, petting, and romance

Homosexuality

Moral, spiritual, and psychological issues associated with sexuality in all the above areas, including abortion

Before the talk, have your child write out the particular questions he or she wants to discuss in the key talk. Be sure to emphasize that no questions in this subject area, however sensitive or tough to answer, are off limits. Nor will any questions, however basic, be considered "dumb."

Meanwhile, you should be preparing your own list of questions that you want to make certain are addressed even if your child doesn't bring them up. Then get your child's questions and add them to your own to create a "master" list you can use to guide this part of your key talk.

The following material covers much more ground than you could possibly tackle in a key talk. But you can draw from the topics presented here to make your own agenda for a conversation that evening, and then follow up with regular conversations about sexuality in the following months. In this chapter we've recommended a few basic subjects to address with your child at some point, and we've listed a few specific questions we hear most often from young people, along with suggested responses.

No book of this scope could fully address all the issues we'll raise in this chapter, but we've included in the back of this volume a list of excellent resources for further study. Some of them are written for parents, and others your children can read for themselves.

Bodily Changes in Adolescence

The most obvious questions young adolescents ask deal with the changes that are taking place in their bodies. These changes may at times be confusing, frustrating, and frightening to children. For some young people, the signs of puberty may even make them wonder whether they have a disease.

Changes in the *male body* you should note in your discussion include these:

Appearance of body hair under arms, on the face, and around genitals
Thickening of hair on arms, legs, and chest
Thickening of muscles
Deepening of voice
Enlargement of the penis and scrotum

Changes in the *female body* you should note include these:

Appearance of body hair under arms and around genitals
Development of breasts to a soft, rounded shape, often accompanied by some sensitivity and soreness

Beginning of menstrual periods

Body fat shaping that causes a rounding of hips and other areas

Slight deepening of voice

Your discussion should emphasize that what's happening in the child's body is normal and necessary for the transition into physical adulthood and the potential for parenthood. You should also point out that the timing and rate of change varies widely among individuals, so your child should not be concerned if his or her bodily changes are occurring earlier or later than the changes in friends.

The Nature of Sexual Intercourse

By the time children are old enough for the key talk, they'll probably already know the basics of sexual intercourse. Nevertheless, they may still have plenty of questions about details that you can help them understand: How long does it last? What does it feel like? Can you have intercourse in different positions? Does intercourse always lead to pregnancy? What makes the difference between intercourse that leads to pregnancy and intercourse that doesn't? Do older people have sex?

You'll probably need to correct a few misconceptions, especially the common myths young people tend to pass around among themselves. Their misinformation may be reflected in questions like these: Is it true that the girl won't get pregnant if she doesn't experience orgasm or if the boy withdraws before ejaculation? Isn't AIDS a problem only for homosexuals and drug users? Don't contraceptives always prevent pregnancy? Aren't people with the most attractive bodies the best lovers? Isn't an unbroken hymen proof that you're a virgin?

Since misinformation from sources other than parents is a common problem for young people, you may need to ask a few questions of your own to find out what your child knows and doesn't know. It might help to start by asking your child to tell *you* the basics of sexual intercourse so you can get an idea of the adjustments you may need to make to his or her picture of sexuality. If your child seems hesitant or embarrassed, help put him or her at ease by talking a little about how much (or little) you knew when you were the same age.

Most likely, you'll need to correct a few misconceptions. . . . Misinformation from sources other than parents is a common problem.

The Reproductive Process

Again, by the age when children are ready for a key talk, they'll probably already know the basics of reproduction. But in this area as well you may need to fill in the gaps in their knowledge or correct some misunderstandings. Your child may ask questions like these: Can a woman get pregnant any time she has intercourse? Why are some babies born with birth defects or born dead? What causes twins? Why don't babies drown in the fluid of the sac that surrounds them in the womb? Why must some women have surgery to deliver a baby? When do people get too old to have babies?

Your child may be especially interested in hearing about your own experience as parents during pregnancy, labor, and delivery, as well as any miscarriages you may have suffered. This would be a good way to introduce discussion in the days to come about subjects like morning sickness, premature birth, the effects of the mother's nutrition on her unborn child, and the role of a husband in supporting his wife during pregnancy. In time you'll also want to tackle related issues like birth control, abortion, and circumcision.

Sexually Transmitted Diseases

Few topics could be of more importance to your child's health than that of sexually transmitted diseases (STDs). More than twenty-five *known* STDs are currently infecting millions of people worldwide. This number includes more than fifteen million per year in the United States alone. Not only does the United States rank highest in the industrialized world for STDs, but each year almost *half* of the fifteen million are under the age of thirty-five. As already discussed in chapter one of this book, promiscuity can debilitate, sterilize, and even kill those who contract such diseases as syphilis, gonorrhea, genital herpes, or AIDS.

Talking about the effects of these diseases may be unpleasant, but your child needs to understand the seriousness of the health risk posed by casual sex. Gonorrhea can lead to arthritis, heart complications, blindness, brain damage, and sterility. In its last stages, syphilis can result in cardiovascular complications, diseases of the brain and spinal cord (including insanity), skin and bone tumors, eye problems, and crippling or killing lesions. Chlamydia can cause genital infection, sterility, and eye disease or pneumonia in infants born to an infected mother.

You should also note in your discussion that the person who contracts an STD has the potential to devastate the health of others as well by infecting sexual partners or, in the case of pregnant women, passing the disease on to a child in the womb—with tragic results.

There are two main types of sexually transmitted diseases. The first is bacterial in nature and can be cured by antibiotics. However, it is important to remember with this type that it is common to experience no symptoms with the infection, and if treatment is not sought and antibiotics administered, the disease continues to silently destroy reproductive organs and spread unknowingly to new partners. It should also be noted that even bacterial infections like gonorrhea, which should respond to antibiotic treatment, are now appearing in new drug-resistant strains.

The second type of STDs is viral in nature and has no known cure at this time. HPV (Human Papillomavirus), also known as genital warts, is this type of viral infection, as is HIV (human immunodeficiency virus). These dangerous infections sometimes have no or only minimal symptoms, so they can be difficult to detect. Hepatitis B attacks the liver, sometimes leading to cirrhosis and cancer. It is one hundred times more contagious than HIV and in most cases is incurable. In addition to the physical devastation, the recurrent pain, severity of symptoms, and the life sentence passed on from these diseases can cause great psychological distress to the carrier as well.

Often, parents can be more concerned about an unwanted pregnancy than the devastating effects of sexually transmitted diseases. But it is important to remember that pregnancy is not a disease and can be dealt with through the wisdom of loving parents and sound counsel. STDs, on the other hand, can destroy and even kill a child. Parents make a terrible mistake when, believing that their child has or is preparing to become sexually active, they encourage the child to use some kind of birth control. This decision to help their child "sin safely" places the child at higher risk statistically for contracting an STD; since they believe their sexual activity is now without consequences, they feel freer to engage in more sexual activity than they might have otherwise.

Be Clear on How STDs Are Transmitted

Parents must ensure that their children understand how easily they can get a sexually transmitted disease. Because some popular magazines and sitcoms, as well as the film and music industries, are encouraging young people to experiment with their sexuality at earlier and earlier ages, they need to know that it takes only one sexual encounter with an infected person to be infected for life, and that any genital contact at all constitutes having sex. The younger a child is when such encounters occur, the more likely it is that he or she will become infected.

Although most STDs are spread during sexual intercourse, children should realize that any contact with body fluids (as is the case with oral sex) can give them an STD. This is because these infections thrive in warm, moist environments in the body such as the genital area, mouth, and throat. It's surprising to learn how many adults are unaware of the fact that STDs can be transmitted through oral sex. It's also shocking to know that many teens do not think "outercourse" (oral sex) is having sex; they think real sex is only when the male's penis enters the female's vagina. But the truth is that even deep kissing is risky for spreading some STDs.

A Few Words About AIDS

We probably know less about AIDS than any other STD, but the soaring rate of its incidence in the current American population requires that our young people learn as much as possible about this killer plague. Here are a few important points your child may not know:

- The opening screen on the website for the American Foundation for AIDS Research reads: "1 in 250 Americans is HIV positive—1 in 500 knows it." A blood test is required to be sure, and sometimes even the blood test fails to show the antibodies that indicate the virus is present. So people who hope to avoid AIDS by having sex only with those who believe they're not infected are literally risking their lives.
- "High-risk groups" are not nearly as significant a factor in infection as "high-risk activities." Though it's presently the case that male homosexuals and intravenous drug users account for the great majority of reported AIDS cases, the virus is also transmitted by heterosexual intercourse. So whether or not a person belongs to a "high-risk group," that person risks infection if he or she engages in high-risk activity.
- Anyone who is infected must be considered infectious. Even when there are no symptoms, a carrier of HIV (which causes AIDS) can transmit the virus to others through high-risk activities.

- AIDS is an extremely painful and debilitating disease. AIDS victims don't suddenly die of the disease; they typically endure a long ordeal of horrible pain and anguish that leads inevitably to death. No moment of sexual pleasure, however thrilling, is worth such a terrible price.

- The risk of infection of HIV through casual contact is minimal, though we presently don't have enough information to say that it's impossible. There are no documented cases today of AIDS being transmitted through deep (French) kissing, but the possibility of that occurrence does exist. The virus has been isolated in saliva, and it's not uncommon for small amounts of blood (which carries the virus) to be present in the mouth from cuts, sores, or bleeding gums.

- The notion of "safe sex" outside of a faithful, monogamous relationship (marriage) is a myth. Condoms may reduce the risk of infection, but they aren't 100 percent effective in that regard. So no form of sexual contact with a possibly infected partner can reasonably be called "safe."

The risk of contracting AIDS increases geometrically with the number of sexual partners. If you have just two sexual partners, and your partners have just two each, and their partners have just two each, you're taking the chance that any one of fourteen people could become infected and pass the disease on to you. Meanwhile, some studies have suggested that the severity of the infection and the speed with which it attacks the body may increase with the number of sexual partners.

Homosexuality

Today, homosexuality has "come out of the closet," with open coverage in the media and a number of popular personalities declaring their homosexual orientation. So our children are more likely than ever to have questions about the phenomenon of same-sex attraction. Their interest may range from simple curiosity to anxious concerns about whether they themselves might have homosexual inclinations.

In the latter category, questions may arise like these: My teacher and I are the same sex, but I have a crush on her/him. Does that mean I'm homosexual? If I have close friends of the same sex, is there a danger our friendship will become homosexual? Does masturbation lead to homosexuality?

Your child needs to know that teenage "crushes" on adult members of the same sex are common. Most adolescents are trying to become independent of their parents even though they feel rather insecure. So they tend to find an older friend who, for a while, can take the place of a parent in providing support while allowing a measure of independence. The attraction to this parent figure may often feel like a romantic "crush."

Your child also needs to know that close same-sex friendships are by no means necessarily a sign of homosexual attraction. Boys may especially be concerned in this regard because our culture has tended to be more accepting of close female bonding than of close male bonding. You can remind your child that the Bible tells us approvingly of several close same-sex friendships that had no sexual element: David and Jonathan, Paul and Timothy, Ruth and Naomi.

David and Jonathan provide an especially clear example of a godly and close male friendship (1 Sam. 18:1–4; 20:17,

23, 40–42; 2 Sam. 1:26). David, the Scripture tells us, loved Jonathan "as he loved himself," and Jonathan returned his love. They entered into a covenant of friendship for life. The Scripture tells us that when they once had to leave each other for an extended time, they cried and hugged each other. Even so, their friendship was not sexual.

At the same time, parents can't automatically rule out the possibility that their child could be experiencing genuine homosexual inclinations. If your child's comments or questions seem to indicate that this is the case, you would do well to seek godly professional help. (More about this possibility in chapter 13, "Special Hurdles.")

God's intent for human sexuality is that it be expressed in the context of a faithful marriage covenant between one man and one woman.

More likely than not, however, your child's questions will focus on the moral implications of homosexuality. In this matter, Christian parents must be clear. A number of voices in today's society are telling our children that homosexuality is a good gift from God, or that the choice of a homosexual lifestyle is a morally neutral option. So we must be sure to establish with our young people the biblical position on the matter.

God's intent for human sexuality is that it be expressed in the context of a faithful marriage covenant between one man and one woman (Gen. 2:18–24; Matt. 19:4–6). A number of scriptural texts clearly teach that homosexuality does not fulfill God's intention in this regard (including Rom. 1:26–27; Lev. 18:22–23; 20:13; Gen. 19:4–5; Judg. 19:22–23; 1 Cor. 6:9–11; 1 Tim. 1:8–11). If your child has some doubts about the biblical standard in this area, you may want to read these scriptural passages together and discuss them.

At the same time, we must help our children distinguish between the homosexual *orientation*, which is a form of brokenness, and homosexual *behavior*, which is sin. Many people have struggled with homosexual inclinations for as long as they can remember, and they cannot honestly identify any actions of their own that have made them that way. The mere fact that they have such an *orientation* may indicate that their normal sexuality has been deeply affected, but that's not the same as sin. Sin becomes a part of the picture when people engage in homosexual *behavior*.

All people are tempted (even Jesus was tempted), but temptation is not the same thing as sin (Heb. 4:15). We sin only when we give in to the temptation. So it's possible for someone to have homosexual tendencies and yet refrain from sin by resisting the temptation, either mentally or physically, to act on his or her sexual feelings—just as it's possible to feel heterosexual temptations and yet avoid sin by resisting them.

This is an important insight for our children because it will help them to treat homosexual persons with compassion instead of condemnation.

Related Moral, Spiritual, and Psychological Issues

As with these questions about homosexuality, we should deal with all our children's concerns about sex not just in biological terms but in moral, spiritual, and psychological terms as well. Commonly, young people will challenge us to defend our understanding of what is right and wrong, or to explain why behaviors that feel so good to their bodies could have destructive results in their souls and spirits.

We should keep in mind as we address these concerns that questions about the basis for our moral standards are not necessarily an attempt to undermine our authority or throw off our restraints. Like all of us, young people need good reasons for making tough choices; in fact, the less they understand about why a standard must be kept, the more likely they are to fail when that standard is tested. So as parents we owe them much more than a simple "Don't do that because it's wrong."

Common questions in this regard are these: If it feels good and doesn't hurt anybody, why shouldn't I do it? How can two people know whether they would be happy together sexually in marriage if they don't try it first? If premarital sex is so wrong, why are so many people doing it? Won't using birth control make it okay? Aren't biblical rules for sex outdated? Is abortion always wrong? Isn't fantasizing about sex all right as long as you don't act out the fantasy? Why is pornography harmful?

Answering such questions will challenge you to think more clearly and deeply yourself about the basis for your moral standards. If you'd like further help in gathering your thoughts for a convincing response to your child, the resources listed at the back of this book should help.

A Few Specific Questions/Suggested Answers

No two young people will have exactly the same list of concerns. But from our experience in counseling our own children as well as others, we have come up with a short list of questions that seem to be asked again and again. With each of those questions, we offer a sample response.

1. Is sex bad in itself?

No—sex is God's wonderful idea. When He created human beings, He made them male and female—sexual creatures who were intended to be joined in marriage and reproduce. When God looked out over what He had created, He saw that it was "very good" (Gen. 1:27–28, 31).

God blesses the sexual relationship in its proper context of a faithful marriage. He has ordained it as a means not just of reproduction, but also of bonding a husband and wife together in a special pleasure of closeness. But outside of marriage, sexual activity is terribly wrong and has tragic emotional and physical consequences.

2. Does the position used in sexual intercourse determine whether or not the woman gets pregnant?

No. Whatever the position of the man or the woman in the sexual act, it's possible for the woman to get pregnant. In fact, pregnancy can occur even if the male hasn't penetrated the vaginal canal. Many couples think that heavy petting is "safe." But if the penis is placed around or near the lips of the vagina, sperm can escape and travel up the vaginal canal.

3. Can a girl get pregnant if she does not go all the way?

Heavy petting that places the penis near the vaginal entrance makes becoming pregnant a possibility. Sperm moves at a high rate of speed and can swim up the vaginal canal from the outside of the vagina. Once there, they go deep inside the vagina to the Fallopian tube and can fertilize the female's egg.

4. What is a "wet dream"? Do both girls and boys have them?

A wet dream, also called a "nocturnal emission," takes place when a person reaches sexual orgasm or release while sleeping. The name "wet dream" comes from the fact that a male ejaculates during such an experience and wets his clothing or bedding with semen. Girls may have a similar experience in which they reach climax while sleeping.

For males, this is the body's way of getting rid of extra semen that has accumulated, and it's perfectly normal. But it's nonetheless important to guard your thoughts about sex during your waking hours, not allowing sensuous material in movies, magazines, books, or television to make undesirable impressions on your memory and imagination—and thus influencing even your dreams in the wrong direction.

5. Is masturbation wrong?

The Bible doesn't deal directly with masturbation (also called "self-stimulation"). But it does talk about the harmful results of the erotic thoughts, mental images, and fantasies that usually accompany masturbation.

Jesus warned us that looking at someone lustfully (even in a magazine) is the equivalent of committing sexual sin in our hearts (Matt. 5:27–29). The book of Proverbs says that as a person "thinks within himself, so he is" (Prov. 23:7 NASB). And the apostle Paul encourages us to think on things that are noble, right, pure, and praiseworthy (Phil. 4:8).

In addition, the practice of masturbation is addictive; in time you feel compelled to do it, even obsessed with doing it, though afterward it leaves you with an empty, unfulfilled feeling.

It's better, we think, to ask God to help you keep your mind free from controlling sexual thoughts. Avoid books, magazines, movies, and pictures that will arouse you sexually, and as far as possible, let the sexual area of your life "sleep" until marriage. The less you masturbate, the less you'll feel pushed to masturbate.

The bad feelings that often come after masturbation may well appear because the act includes only yourself, while an orgasm was intended by God to come as the result of shared lovemaking between a husband and wife. A sense of guilt may also mean that the Holy Spirit is convicting you to clean up your thought life. If your sexual passions far outweigh your desire to please God, think about these words from the Bible:

> It is God's will that you should be holy; that you should avoid sexual immorality; that each of you should learn to control his own body in a way that is holy and honorable, not in passionate lust like the heathen, who do not know God. . . . For God did not call us to be impure, but to live a holy life.
>
> 1 Thessalonians 4:3–5, 7 NIV

Or, as another Bible version puts it, we're called "to dedicate ourselves to the most thorough purity" (AMP).

We don't think you can do that and still be addicted to masturbation.

> **6. How do you know whether a guy is a virgin? Why isn't the importance of virginity emphasized for guys as well as for girls? Can a guy tell if you're not a virgin?**

There's no physical way to tell whether a guy is a virgin, as there often is with a girl. He has to tell you himself.

In God's eyes, virginity until marriage is just as important for men as for women. But the world typically has a double standard in that area. Mothers and fathers are intended by God to share the responsibility of caring for a child. But because women actually carry the child physically in their womb and men do not, men can walk away from a sexual encounter and shun their share of the responsibility. As a result, the world has tended to place a greater responsibility on women in matters of fertility.

When a girl has her first sexual experience, a partial covering at the opening of the vagina, called the *hymen,* may be broken, sometimes accompanied by slight bleeding. But this would not provide a foolproof way for a guy to tell whether a girl is a virgin.

> **7. If you know that your boyfriend has had sex with other girls, is it all right for you to have sex with him as well?**

Sex outside of marriage is sin, and sin separates us from God. It's important to please God in all our relationships, not allowing others to cause us to do anything that might hinder our relationship with God—who should be our best friend. "The body is not meant for sexual immorality, but for the Lord" (1 Cor. 6:13 NIV).

If you know your boyfriend has been promiscuous, he's probably not a good influence on you; he may tempt you to become one of his many sexual "conquests." His lifestyle also increases the chances that he has already acquired an STD and can pass it to you. Remember that even without vaginal intercourse, STDs can be passed through body fluids and contact with infected genitals. The Bible asks: "Can two walk together, except they be agreed?" (Amos 3:3). So if the two of you can't agree that all sexual activity outside of marriage is sin, you should end the relationship.

8. Why don't I have stronger sexual feelings for my boy/girlfriend?

You may well be "sexually asleep." That is, your sexual feelings may not have been aroused prematurely by certain music, movies, or sensual behavior the way others' feelings have been. You can receive the condition of being "sexually asleep" as God's gracious provision for someone who is not yet ready to marry.

Another deterrent to those feelings may well be that you have considered the penalties of sexual indulgence outside of marriage and have been convinced that the sin simply isn't worth the price. That too is a healthy place to be. Be careful not to listen to Satan's lie that a lack of sexual desire means something is wrong with you.

Finally, keep in mind that different people come into sexual awareness and desire at different ages. You're unique, so don't let the biological clocks of other people control you.

9. If you were in a relationship that involved sex before you became a Christian, how do you stop having sex now that you're a Christian?

We'd suggest these steps:

- Openly discuss the problem and identify the behavior as sin in God's eyes.
- Make an agreement that your lives now will be lived to please God. If your partner is not a Christian and will not agree to obey God's Word, then break off the relationship.
- Dates should be well planned so that all situations where you would be alone together are avoided. Care should be taken that an evening involving a romantic movie doesn't become a catalyst for a sexual encounter. Try group dates.
- Avoid deep (French) kissing and body contact that can generate sexual excitement.
- Pray for each other daily, especially before and after each date. Keep God in the center of your friendship.
- If you should fail to keep your covenant with God to remain sexually pure, it's better to dissolve the relationship than to risk further sexual involvement. You might try separating for several months until you both are stronger in the Lord.

10. How do you recognize the person that God has for you?

The ability to recognize the person who's meant to be your spouse comes in much the same way as other kinds of discernment. Sometimes we seem to have an immediate knowledge of what's right, but at other times we simply grow in our awareness over a period of time.

In this area as in others, how well we know the voice of the Lord depends on the quality of our relationship with Him. As we walk with God, He leads us by His Spirit. Remember: "The steps of a good man are ordered by the Lord: and he delighteth in his way" (Ps. 37:23).

These are the most common questions we've encountered among young people in key talks and in other frank discussions about sex. As we said before, you won't be able to cover all these subjects thoroughly in one evening's conversation. But the key talk can become one of many honest discussions with your child so that he or she learns to make a habit of talking over with you any questions about sexuality that may arise. Just keep this chapter handy for your child's ongoing "homeschool" in sex education.

Points to Remember

- You can prepare for the question-and-answer portion of the key talk by reviewing ahead of time some of the most common questions asked.

- Ask your child to provide you with his or her own list of questions a week before the talk, and then add to that list the issues you will want to make sure are addressed.

- Topics of discussion during the key talk and in later conversations might include these:

  Bodily changes in adolescence
  Sexual intercourse

The reproductive process
Sexually transmitted diseases
Masturbation and petting
Dating and romance
Homosexuality
The spiritual and moral implications of all these
issues

- For more information, check the resources listed in
the back of this book.

5

How to Have a Key Talk

You've prepared yourself for the big night. You've studied the biblical meaning of a covenant so you can share it with your child. You've gone over some of the questions your child is most likely to ask, thinking carefully about how you will respond. Now it's time to make some concrete plans for a key talk and carry them out.

Making Plans

The first thing to take care of is choosing a ring, because it may take some weeks to find or create the one you want. As we mentioned before, we have found the "key" symbolism to hold great significance, so we encourage you to choose a ring that somehow incorporates that symbol in its design—perhaps through an engraving. You may also want to have the date engraved inside. The ring need not be an expensive piece of jewelry, but neither should it look cheap or fragile, because it represents a precious and enduring commitment.

Next, think about how you'll "bill" the event. Your own attitude will make a great difference in your child's anticipation of the night. Whatever you do to enhance the specialness of the meeting pays great dividends when the evening finally comes.

First, you'll want to build some excitement and even some mystery. A few weeks before the event, tell your child that you want to have a date with him or her in order to hold one of the most important talks of his or her life. Label it a "key talk" and let them begin to guess just what it might involve. Maybe you'll want to send your child a formal invitation, either handwritten on fancy stationery or in a nice card. Or punctuate your more-than-usual interest in the event by calling your child at an unusual time to issue the invitation—during the day while you're at the office, or long-distance when you're on a business trip.

One especially nice touch is to send a child a bouquet of flowers with the invitation. In addition, Dad may want to send a card to his daughter saying his heart will be with her and Mom on that special night; Mom can do the same for a son who's having the key talk with Dad.

Between the time you issue the invitation and have the date, you can build anticipation and show your own excitement by leaving an occasional note around the house: in the medicine cabinet or toiletry drawer, on the bathroom mirror or refrigerator, in your child's schoolbooks, or on his or her pillow or dinner plate. Little Post-it Notes are great for this. Just say on the note something like "Can't wait till our key talk," "Only five days till our key talk," or "Are you getting ready for our key talk?"

Note in your invitation that dress for the evening will be the very best you have. As we mentioned before, people dress up for the most important events of their lives, and this night's attire should rank right up there with the clothes you might wear to attend a symphony concert, a high school graduation, or a wedding. If the budget allows, you might even let your child buy a new small article of clothing to wear that evening—a scarf or a necktie, for example. But don't be concerned if finances won't stretch that far; the money spent should not be the focus of the night.

Even so, if your budget is tight, you'll probably need to plan ahead if you want the night to be special in every way. You don't have to go to the most expensive place in town, but you do want the atmosphere to be pleasant, low-key, and relatively private. Be prepared if possible to order anything on the menu—even appetizers and dessert. Teens have big appetites!

Let your child know that this will be the time to ask any questions about sexuality and romance, no holds barred.

If that kind of meal out requires saving for a few weeks, then remember that your financial sacrifice will send a clear message to your child: "They mean it when they call this a once-in-a-lifetime event." If you already know that your child has a favorite restaurant that would suit the occasion, that place may be your best bet.

We should note that even though we're describing the key talk in a dining setting, it doesn't have to take place in a restaurant. We know of one father who set aside a weekend to take his son on a camping trip for his key talk. One mother we know took her daughter for an overnight stay at a nice hotel. The possibilities are endless—just keep in mind that whatever location you choose, you should have adequate time alone with your child in an environment that says loud and clear, *This is a once-in-a-lifetime occasion.*

Early on, you may not want to reveal the content of the key talk. In fact, the mystery is part of the excitement, so reveal as few details as possible. Younger children in the family can be told that their brother or sister is going out for an extremely special occasion. Older siblings who have already had a key talk should keep what they know about it to themselves. Let curiosity add to the fun as your child speculates for a couple of weeks about what you're up to.

Next, set a specific date and time. Weekends are probably best, because your child won't be distracted by thoughts of homework or other responsibilities, and you won't have to be home early because of early rising the next day for school. And it's better to start early in the evening and leave the schedule open-ended so that there's no need to rush.

Perhaps a week before the big date, pull your child aside privately to let him or her in on the overall content of the conversation. Again, refrain from giving too many details, such as the covenant and the ring; just let your child know that this will be the time to ask any questions about sexuality and romance, no holds barred. That way he or she will have some time to think ahead about questions to ask or issues to raise.

Whatever setting you choose, you should be thinking ahead as well about how you want the conversation to flow throughout the key talk. In the following pages we'll recommend a sample agenda for an order of "events." But you can create your own agenda, or rearrange the items on ours. We do urge you, however, to save the presentation of the ring and the sealing of the covenant until the end. Our experience has been that these are the highlight of the evening.

A Sample Agenda

In general, a key talk should include the following elements:

1. A relaxed and intimate meal together, eaten without any sense of time pressure and uninterrupted by distractions that could steal your attention from your child.
2. A conversation that establishes clearly the beauty and value of sexuality and virginity until marriage.
3. A question-and-answer session that allows your child to ask any questions or raise any concerns about sexuality, with no questions considered "dumb" or off limits.
4. A discussion of the meaning of a covenant, with special application to the covenant you will be asking the child to make that night.
5. Prayer for your child's future spouse.
6. The presentation of the key ring, with an explanation of its significance.
7. Signing the covenant and sealing it with prayer.

Each of these elements contributes a critical dimension to the key talk.

As we've said, many prefer a special restaurant setting. If that is your choice, we'd like to offer some simple guidelines.

The meal. If possible, your table should be away from heavy traffic areas. A booth is nice, because it's both quiet and private—the less noise and the fewer distractions, the better. If necessary, call ahead to reserve a particular table.

We should note, however, that when Richard and Jonathan had their key talk, Richard did call ahead for a private table, but to no avail. A mix-up in the reservation list left them eating in one of the most public places in the restaurant.

Even so, when Richard raised the concern with the hostess, God reminded him that there was something to be said for having the key talk in a more public setting: If Jonathan were unwilling to hold his dad's hands and pray in public, how would he be able to withstand the peer pressure against keeping his covenant with God?

A letter we received from one of the many couples who used the key talk idea with their kids reminded us that if our attempts to plan these important details go awry, God is still in control. In fact, He may have overriding concerns. In this case, the mother and her daughter were given the private booth they asked for. But the waitress provided them with more attentive service than they wanted, and they felt constantly interrupted.

On the table was a copy of a magazine with an article Richard had written about the key talk, for the mom to use as reference. Again and again, the waitress returned to the table and slowly refilled their water glasses, eyeing the magazine and hearing bits of the conversation. Finally she asked how she could get a copy of that issue.

They gave her their own copy to keep, and she was thrilled. "Thank you so much," she said. "I have three teenage daughters at home." Despite all the interruptions, the mother and daughter were happy to know that their key talk was already having positive repercussions beyond their own family.

If possible, plan an evening without time constraints. Keep a relaxed pace and allow your child ample time to talk and think about the issues at hand. Avoid looking at your watch—in fact, you're probably better off leaving your watch at home for the evening to avoid the temptation altogether.

Finally, be sure to give your child your undivided attention for the entire evening. Speaking to acquaintances who might be dining at a table nearby or having long chats with the server give your child the impression that others are more important than he or she is. So act as if there's no one else in the restaurant but the two of you.

Conversation about values. As you begin the evening's conversation, state the focus briefly and directly. You might want to say something like this:

> "Anna, when I was your age, my parents didn't talk to me about sex. I wish they had, because it would have helped me through some hard times. That's why I want us to have this conversation tonight. Being a teenager isn't easy, but we can walk through these years together. I really want to be a friend you know will always be there for you. You will never be alone."

Or here's another approach:

> "Jonathan, tonight is your night to ask any questions you might have about your body, sexuality, romance, or the opposite sex. I may not be able to give you all the answers, but I'll do my best. I remember how I felt at your age, and I needed to know some things."

At this point, you might want to share some amusing or at-the-time embarrassing experience that you may have had as a teen. Maybe your first date was a disaster, or you got slapped the first time you kissed a girl. Perhaps your voice changed so rapidly in puberty that it cracked whenever you tried to speak in public, or your mother turned crimson with embarrassment the day you asked her the meaning of that word you read on the school rest room wall.

Talk some about what life was like when you were a teenager. Be honest about some of the pressures, the uncertainties, the frustrations. You may want to note whether you had an adult confidant who was willing to talk over these things with you, and what it meant to you to have (or lack) that confidant.

These reminiscences should take the edge off any anxiety you or your child might be experiencing and make the evening more enjoyable for both of you.

One priority of the ensuing conversation should be to discuss the beauty and value of sexuality and maintaining virginity until marriage. To avoid a talk that majors on rules and negatives, you need to begin with the bigger picture, a context that emphasizes how God Himself made us sexual beings—so we can receive our sexuality from Him as a beautiful and precious gift. The Bible says that God saw *everything* He had created, and it was very good (Genesis 1).

Your child needs to know that the new feelings and bodily changes he or she is experiencing are in themselves natural, clean, and holy. Once you've made this point, you might want to use yourself as an example of how insecure you felt as you went through changes in height, shape, voice pitch, and other signs of puberty. Emphasize that entering adolescence is a time of emotional as well as physical change that may sometimes be confusing.

This approach to the subject allows you to talk about the social and moral dimensions of sexuality. Because God created us, He knows what's best for us, and His "manufacturer's instruction manual"—the Bible—provides the most reliable guide for a healthy and moral life. Referring to a few key Scriptures (see the suggestions in the back of this book), talk about God's insistence that He created sex to be reserved for marriage. Note that within marriage, sex provides for reproduction to take place within the secure and nurturing environment of the family. It also creates a deep emotional and social bonding that powerfully undergirds a lifelong mutual commitment.

By the same token, your child must realize that sex outside of marriage provides none of these benefits. Instead, it devastates the emotions and the conscience, leaving people who engage in it with feelings of shame, low self-esteem, and disillusionment with romance and marriage. Because our Creator never intended us to engage in sex outside of marriage, when we do so we sin against Him, against our sex partner, and against ourselves and our own bodies.

You will probably want to add to the discussion some of the sobering statistics cited in the first chapter of this book. Though this information is unpleasant and even frightening, it can create a realistic and healthy fear of promiscuity's dire physical consequences.

The most important point in all this is that your child should reserve his or her precious sexual gift—physical, emotional, and social—for the future spouse. Only in the context of marriage will his or her sexuality find its divine purpose fulfilled.

Tell your child that God knows his or her future and has wonderful plans ahead. God cares that we marry the right person and will help us find that person. What greater gift could your child give someone on their wedding night than to say, "I've saved myself all these years just for you, because I believe you're God's one-of-a-kind gift to me!"

Your child will most likely be hearing the "everyone's doing it" excuse, so you'll have to correct that misinformation. Remind him or her that throughout this nation and in other parts of the world, millions of young people are choosing to remain sexually pure and keeping themselves for a future spouse.

As you pursue these issues, you may come up against several challenges. Your child may inquire about your own premarital sexual history. There may be some questions about the validity or relevance of "old-fashioned" biblical standards. Your son or daughter may even have already lost his or her virginity. For that reason, we have included a chapter later in this book, "Special Hurdles," to help you deal with these possibilities. You'll want to be sure to read it before you have your key talk.

In any case, let this be a time when you and your child can have a heart-to-heart discussion of the moral and spiritual matters involved in handling our sexuality. Even if some of the moments are difficult or uncomfortable, don't avoid any issue you know to be important—your child's physical, emotional, and spiritual health could be in the balance. You can trust the Holy Spirit to be there with you, counseling you with wisdom and persuading your child of the truth.

Answering questions. In the previous chapter on preparing for the key talk, we discussed some of the questions your child is most likely to have about human biology, sexuality, romance, and the opposite sex. This is the point in your key talk when you will probably want to begin addressing those questions. You and your child may even want to bring to the talk a written list of questions to be answered.

Young teens may be taken aback to hear some of what you have to say. Some children, for example, are surprised to discover that sex is part of their mom and dad's relationship.

Meet their surprise with positive assurance. At the same time, convey a confident, unembarrassed attitude when responding to unexpected queries. The tone of what you say will teach your child at least as much as the content of what you say.

The diagrams and glossary in this book may be helpful as you respond to your child's questions. If you or your child need further information, refer to the books listed in the bibliography. (We recommend *The Wonder of Me* by Ruth S. Taylor, MD, MPH, and Ann Nerbun, RN, MSN—see the resource list on page 188.)

By placing purity in the context of a faithful, intimate relationship with a personal God, you help your child get beyond mere rules and resolutions.

Discussing the covenant. The next element of the key talk has already been discussed at length as part of your preparation (see chapter 3), because it required some Bible study on your part. Now that study should pay off as you spend some time talking with your child about what the Scriptures have to say.

This portion of your conversation allows you to focus on the spiritual aspect of the commitment your child needs to make. By placing sexual purity in the context of a faithful, intimate relationship with a personal God, you help your child get beyond mere rules and resolutions. He or she can gain an understanding of the covenant as a living bond that makes God's power and grace available to live with integrity.

Prayer for the future spouse. Take a few moments now to talk about how you can intercede for your child's future husband or wife. You can ask for that person to be matured, protected, and guided in the years to come. Such prayer will nourish your child's faith in God's control of the future and provide the understanding that his or her job is to trust God's perfect wisdom for the best life that He has in store for them.

This element of the key talk should form the beginning of an established habit for both your child and you as you join him or her in the days to come in ongoing prayer for that special person. For that reason, we will discuss it more completely in one of our later chapters on how to follow up on the key talk.

Presentation of the key ring. Before you leave home to go out for the key talk, be sure you have the key ring in your pocket or purse; in all the excitement, you might forget! A good time to present it is after you've discussed the meaning of a covenant.

Explain the symbolism of this piece of jewelry. Tell why you chose this particular ring and why it's called a "key ring." Remind your child that in the Old Testament, covenants were often sealed with a special token as a reminder of the commitment, and offer this ring as a similar token of the covenant he or she is about to make. Finally, encourage your child that the ring is to be worn with pride and faithfulness during the difficult teen and young adult years, until his or her wedding night, when the future spouse will receive it as a precious gift.

Signing and sealing the covenant. After your child receives the ring as a token of the commitment, it's time to share a few quiet moments together praying aloud to seal the covenant. It may feel awkward at first to pray in a public setting, with table servers whizzing by, knowing that others might be watching or listening. But as we mentioned before, if your teen has the courage to pray in front of others, he or she will also be more likely to have the courage to say no to premarital sex.

By your example on this night and at other times, you are teaching your child to stand alone against the pressures of our society. If your child senses that you are not ashamed to pray publicly, he or she will be encouraged to share your confidence.

Have your child pray first. Be sure to cover the following points:

1. A promise to remain sexually pure until marriage.
2. A request for grace to keep the covenant.
3. A request for grace, protection, and guidance for the future husband or wife.

After your child prays, you should pray aloud as well, affirming and agreeing with what has been said. Some parents may be uncomfortable with this, but the truth is, your prayer is critical to the success of the key talk. Why? First, it reinforces in your child's mind what you are expecting. More important, the faithful prayers of godly parents have a profound effect on our children.

You may also want to write the covenant out in some way so that your child can sign it as a black-and-white declaration of his or her promise or use the reproducible certificate found on page 77 that has a brief statement of the child's promise, a Bible verse telling of God's own covenant faithfulness, a place for the date, and a place for both child and parent to sign.

Finally, to cap off the evening, you may want to read your son or daughter a letter that we read to our youngest, Jonathan, at the end of his key talk. It was written by Dr. James Dobson, who had befriended our son when he was little and who had graciously agreed to add his own words of encouragement to the evening. We found that it beautifully summed up many of our thoughts and concerns.

Then just fill in the blank with your own child's name in the greeting. Here's the letter:

Dear _____,

I've been invited to participate in this discussion by way of a letter. I was asked to say a few things about purity—sexual purity—though I don't suppose there's much I can tell you that you haven't heard before.

I'm sure your parents have taught you well. But I want to encourage you to act on what you already know. Believe me, it's worth it to save sex for marriage and keep yourself pure for the man/woman God wants you to spend your life with. The Lord designed it that way for good reasons. Plenty of people who disregarded His plan in that area will tell you how much they regret it.

You're going to need more of this kind of encouragement in the days to come. It's one thing to know what's right. Living by it is something else. Over the next few years, you'll probably face pressure to change or compromise your values—pressure from your friends, advertising, television and movies, and a hundred other sources. You may even find yourself in situations where it could be easy to yield to sexual temptation.

One of the best ways of fighting back is learning to like yourself. If you feel good about you, you'll have the confidence to take a stand—even if you're the only one! Just remember who you are and what your parents have taught you. There's real strength in knowing that God loves you and has a purpose for your life!

But if you feel inferior to others, it will be that much easier to let them press you into their mold. Don't do it! The rest of your life is ahead of you, and it's worth fighting for. I hope this helps, (name). I'm sure your dad or mom will have more to say on this. You're a lucky person to have parents who care about you so much! Take advantage of their wisdom and be encouraged by their love. God bless you!

What better way to conclude one of the most important conversations you and your child will ever have?

Points to Remember

A key talk should include the following elements:

- A relaxed and intimate meal together.
- A conversation that establishes clearly the beauty and value of sexuality and virginity until marriage.
- A question-and-answer session that allows your child to ask any questions or raise any concerns about sexuality, with no questions considered "dumb" or off limits.
- A discussion of the meaning of the covenant you will be asking the child to make that night.
- Prayer for your child's future spouse.
- The presentation of the key ring.
- Signing the covenant and sealing it with prayer.

FOR WEDLOCK ONLY
"A Promise With a Ring to It"

Covenant

Lord, realizing that my body is yours and that you live in me, I ask you this day for your help to keep myself sexually pure until marriage.

I promise to keep this covenant and to resist any temptation to break it.

I ask that you will also help my mate-to-be. Keep that person in your love and protect him/her from all danger.

In your perfect time, bring us together in such a way that we will know for sure that we were meant for one another.

Lord, you always keep your promises. Help me to keep mine.

> *"Know therefore that the Lord thy God, he is God, the faithful God, which keepeth covenant and mercy with them that love him and keep his commandments to a thousand generations."*
> *Deuteronomy 7:9*

Dated this _____ day of _____ 20_____

_____ / _____
Signature   Witness

6

Praying for Your Child's Future Spouse

As a child, Richard was encouraged by his mother to pray for his wife-to-be. The notion admittedly seemed a little strange at first. How do you pray for someone you've probably never even met?

Richard didn't have a clue about who his future wife might be. But he nevertheless took his mom's advice. He faithfully asked the Lord over a period of years to protect and guide that bride-to-be and to bring them together in His perfect time.

When Renée finally came along, it didn't take long for him to discover that she was the woman for whom he'd been praying for so long. Two weeks after the first meeting came the engagement. That was more than twenty-five wonderful years ago.

Never once have we questioned whether or not God had answered Richard's prayer. Our confidence that the Lord brought us together has been a source of strength during difficult times and a constant reminder that each of us is a gift from God to the other. And it all began with Richard's prayers for someone he had never met.

The time you spend praying for your child's future spouse during the key talk can become the first of many such meaningful conversations with God. No Christian who has discovered the unmatched power of prayer would doubt that regular intercession for this future addition to the family can make all the difference in your child's life. The Lord will respond to your prayers with protection and guidance, growth and maturity for the young person who will one day walk the aisle with your own precious son or daughter.

> **Praying with your child for his or her future mate cultivates faith that God is in control of his or her future, and somewhere out there, a special someone may be waiting. . . . Being prepared for the day when God will bring them together.**

Another benefit of praying with your child for his or her future mate is the faith it cultivates that God is in control of their future, and somewhere out there, a special someone may be waiting. Just as the ring is a constant reminder of the key talk covenant, so consistent prayer reinforces in the mind of a child that the covenant is real and must be fulfilled by faith.

The awareness that God has a wonderful plan for his or her life that may include marriage brings home the possibility that this person already exists and is being prepared for the day when God will bring them together. That kind of awareness will provide in your child an additional source of strength when he or she is tempted to compromise sexual standards.

Yet another benefit of praying with your child for the partner-to-be is the opportunity it will give the two of you to discuss your child's expectations for a spouse. As you encourage your child to pray specifically, you'll inevitably have to talk about what specifically to pray for. For example, if your child tends to pray with a certain list of talents or physical traits in mind, rather than character qualities, you may need to talk further about what's most important in a spouse.

How to Pray

How should you pray? Here are a few suggestions:

1. Both you and your child should make prayer for a future mate a part of your daily personal prayer times, right alongside prayer for your family members.
2. In addition to individual prayer, you and your child should also pray about the matter together on a regular basis.
3. Pray for God's perfect will to be worked out in the child's life, and if His will includes marriage, pray that God will be preparing both people for that special day.
4. Encourage your child to pray for the future spouse as he or she would pray for a best friend. Whatever your child would pray for someone very near and dear whom he or she already knows and loves would make an appropriate prayer for the future mate as well.
5. Pray for your future son- or daughter-in-law as you would pray for your own children now. Whatever

concerns you may have today as a parent, take on
those concerns for your future in-law as well.

6. Pray for the young person's spiritual life and development. Ask God to allow him or her to have a vital
relationship with Jesus that's constantly growing
deeper and richer. Pray for appropriate role models, mentors, and teachers to catalyze and direct the
young person's growth.

7. Assume that the future mate is about the same age
as your child, with many of the same problems and
challenges, hopes and fears, frustrations and achieve-
ments. Whatever your child has to pray about for
him or herself can become a prayer for the future
partner as well: physical, emotional, and spiritual
health and protection; grace to succeed in school and
other settings; healthy, strong family relationships;
and wisdom in making life choices.

8. Pray for the person's parents, that God will give them
grace and wisdom in rearing their child. Pray for
adequate financial provision for the family.

9. Encourage your child to pray especially that God
will keep the other person sexually pure, just as your
child prays that for him or herself.

10. Ask God to cultivate in the other young person the
fruit of His Spirit, even as He does the same for your
child.

Character Qualities

Long ago, the Hebrew patriarch Abraham sent his chief
servant as an envoy to another country to find a bride for
his son Isaac. Abraham's only request was that the woman

must come from among his own relatives back in his native land. So the envoy went to the town where his master's extended family lived and waited at the well as the women of the town came out to draw water.

What was the envoy's strategy? He knew that not just any woman would do for Isaac, who was the inheritor of God's promises for a great and chosen nation. Isaac needed a woman of good character—a spouse who had a godly servant's heart.

> **The key is to get your child thinking about the most important qualities for lifelong partners to cultivate.**

So the envoy prayed that the Lord would point out the right woman by revealing her heart. He asked that his master's future daughter-in-law might show herself worthy by giving him water and offering even to water his camels. Then before the prayer was even finished, God answered: Out came Rebekah, Abraham's grandniece, and did just what the envoy had asked for (Gen. 24:1–27).

Rebekah's story teaches us an important lesson even today. The happiest, healthiest marriages result when each of the partners has a servant's heart—a heart like our Lord Jesus.

As you and your child pray, you have an excellent opportunity to explore together the character qualities of a servant's heart that go into building a strong marriage. As these are identified, your child can pray specifically for each one to be developed in the future mate as well as in him or herself.

Not surprisingly, the qualities necessary for a healthy, mature marital relationship are the same as those that make a healthy, mature individual. To identify those traits, we can turn to the Scriptures. In a number of passages there we're told what makes godly men and women who consistently display the character of Christ as spouses and parents.

A good place to start in your child's search for admirable character qualities is the apostle Paul's list of the fruit of the Spirit: love, joy, peace, patience, kindness, goodness, faithfulness, gentleness, and self-control (Gal. 5:22–23 NIV). Each of these traits probably merits its own conversation as you and your child talk about what these terms mean and how each kind of fruit would benefit a marriage.

Other qualities you might discuss, and some Scripture verses that refer to them, are these:

Humility (Phil. 2:3–4)
Wisdom (James 3:17–18)
Mercy (Col. 3:13)
Integrity (Prov. 11:3)
Courage (Deut. 31:6)
Cheerfulness (Prov. 15:15)
Generosity (Prov. 11:25)

Of course, you and your child can expand the list as you desire. The key is to get your child thinking about the most important qualities for lifelong partners to cultivate.

Traits Other Than Character Qualities

A married couple we know tells the story of how, before they'd ever met, each of them had a list of characteristics they wanted in a spouse. Neither one had ever written the list down, but it was subtly etched in the back of their minds, filtering all their perceptions about who might or might not be an appropriate candidate for marriage.

Both were Christians, so both included on their lists some of the character qualities that make for godliness and a happy marriage. But *he* was a vocal soloist, so near the top of his list was the requirement that she have a beautiful voice to sing duets with him. Meanwhile, *she* had been a recreation major in college, so high in her priorities was a man with athletic prowess.

Then they met each other, and the rest is history. The funny thing is that, as they put it, he can't carry a football and she can't carry a tune. She's no musician and he's no athlete. But they'll soon be celebrating their twelfth anniversary, and today they can only laugh at those little secret lists they once kept in their hearts.

Your child may very well have a similar mental list tucked away in a corner of his or her dreams. If so, you'd do well to talk it over. Conversations about what's really important and what's not can save your child some frustration and help your child focus on important character qualities in his or her own development.

Our children may assume that they need to find someone much like themselves in order to live together comfortably. To a certain extent, that's true, especially with regard to finding someone who shares their *values*. In addition, certain personality types do appear to be more compatible in marriage, and it never hurts for a husband and wife to have some common background and interests.

Nevertheless, in our own experience and in the experience of countless married couples we've counseled, we've found that in a marriage, *complementary* is at least as important as *commonality*. That's simply to say that the differences between spouses can fit together nicely, with one person's strengths making up for the other's weaknesses. The differences also add "spice" to a relationship; two people exactly alike would probably lead a rather dull life as husband and wife!

With these insights in mind, your child may need to recognize that you can't always tell ahead of time what kind of personality or background will make just the right partner for life. To get some of the potentially unrealistic expectations out in the open, you might take some time to ask your child a few questions like these:

1. Are you praying for a partner with a list of particular personality traits (as opposed to character qualities) in mind? (Examples: outgoing, adventurous, aggressive, energetic, settled, submissive, independent, conservative, traditional, quiet, decisive.)
2. Does your list of preferable traits for a spouse include physical traits?
3. Does your list include special talents, skills, or interests? (Examples: musical, artistic, mechanical, or athletic ability; desire to travel; great intellect or knowledge; domestic skills.)
4. How important do you think these non-character traits are for the success of your future marriage?
5. Do you think your expectations are realistic?
6. How will you feel if the person you marry turns out not to match the list?
7. If your future spouse is praying the same way, what kind of list would he or she have to draw up for you to match it? That is, what personality traits, talents, skills, and interests would you be bringing into the relationship?

8. As you pray, are you assuming that your future spouse will come from a particular background—economic, cultural, ethnic? Are you limiting God by your assumptions?

9. Do you believe God Himself has already picked out one particular person for you to marry? Or are you praying for that person whom God knows He will one day allow you to choose for yourself?

10. How do you expect to recognize the person you've been praying for?

11. Do you expect your parents to recognize the right person for you as well? Do you consider your parents' approval of your choice to be one requirement for engagement?

Be alert to any details of your child's "prayer list" that might indicate a faulty view of marriage or a low sense of self-esteem. For example, a child might be hoping for "someone who'll take care of me" or "somebody who'll look so good, I'll be proud to walk down the street with her." Such prayers reveal a few areas of misunderstanding and faulty self-perceptions that need to be discussed.

While you're at it, you may also want to talk about some good and bad reasons for choosing a particular person as a mate. Some bad reasons to discuss might include "she knows how to turn me on physically" or "I'm getting older, and no one else may come along."

You and your child may not agree completely on the answers to all the questions above. But the discussion they generate will challenge each of you to think in some new ways about your child's developing values and hopes for the future.

Pray the Scriptures

If we don't always know the kind of mate that will fit someone best, how can we know we're praying according to God's will as we pray for our child's future spouse? One way is to "pray the Scriptures."

What we mean is this: You can take passages from the Bible that refer to God's desires for your child and for his or her future spouse, and then paraphrase those passages in the words of your own prayer. For example, Psalm 128 is a song of blessing on godly families. You can pray the words of this psalm in a way something like this (based here on the NIV translation):

> Lord, may my child and his/her future mate always fear you and walk in your ways (v. 1).
>
> May they eat the fruit of their labor, with blessings and prosperity (v. 2).
>
> May they be like fruitful vines within their home, and their children like young plants around their table (v. 3).
>
> May they live to see their children's children, and live in peace (v. 6).

Author Quin Sherrer, in a wonderful book called *How to Pray for Your Children*, takes a similar approach to praying the Scriptures when she offers a "Prayer for My Daughter's Future Partner":

> Lord, may he love the Lord with all his heart, soul, mind and strength, and Jesus as his personal Lord and Savior (Mark 12:29; Rom. 10:9).

May he love his wife with a faithful, undying love for as long as they both shall live (Matt. 19:5–6).

May he recognize his body as the temple of the Holy Spirit and treat it wisely (1 Cor. 16:19, 20). May he be healthy, able to work and support a family (1 Tim. 6:8).

May he have an admirable goal in life (Matt. 6:33).

May he use his talents wisely and release his wife to use her God-given talents also. May their talents complement one another. May they enjoy doing things together (Matt. 25:1, 14–30).

May he establish their home in accordance with God's prescribed order in Ephesians 5:20–28.

May he be strong in mind. May the two of them be compatible intellectually (2 Cor. 13:11; 1 Tim. 1:7).

May he be a good money manager (1 Tim. 5:8; 6:10).

Lord, bring this partner into my daughter's life in Your perfect timing. May she be so in love with him and he with her and both of them in love with You, Oh God, that there will be no doubt that You created them for each other as long as they both shall live.

In Jesus' name, Amen.[1]

With so many scriptural passages relating to marriage and godly character, the possibilities for praying the Scriptures in this way are endless. The long-term benefits as God answers those prayers will be endless too.

One Last Caution

A final thought: We've talked about trying not to pray in a way that builds unrealistic expectations about the future spouse's temperament, skills, and background. But even when we concentrate on praying about character qualities, we can fall into a similar "expectation trap."

We heard about one couple's argument in bed one night, in which the wife began telling her husband all the wonderful virtues and other qualities she thought he had before she married him. Obviously, she concluded, she'd been sadly mistaken.

Unruffled, her husband listened quietly, then turned over to go to sleep. "Only one person could ever meet your expectations," he said sleepily. "And He died on a cross between two thieves."

When we pray, we should try to avoid establishing in our minds an ideal but unrealistic image of a perfect spouse who is mature and Christlike in every way. That's an expectation our future son- or daughter-in-law could never live up to. So instead of praying for perfection, it's better to focus on praying for the *process* that will shape the character of our child's partner-to-be.

That process can be painful. For Rebekah to demonstrate the character qualities needed in Isaac's future bride, she had to endure the heat and hard work of watering those camels. The same is true for your child and his or her future partner: To develop the character that will make them ready for each other, they'll have to make it through some difficult tests and challenges.

Those tests are sure to be going on even now. So your future in-law no doubt needs your prayers, and the prayers of your child, today. We need not pray that God would spare him or her from all adverse circumstances. But we can certainly pray that He would grant the grace to develop godly character as he or she grows in the days and years to come.

Points to Remember

- Praying with your child for his or her future spouse has at least three benefits:

  1. It brings God's power to bear on the life of your future son- or daughter-in-law as he or she faces the challenges of youth.
  2. It brings home to your child the reality of the future spouse's existence as a real person for whom he or she is staying pure.
  3. It gives you an opportunity to discuss your child's expectations for a spouse.

- Pray regularly for your future in-law the way you pray for your own child.
- Help your child understand the character qualities desirable in a life partner so he or she can pray for these qualities to be developed in the future spouse and in him or herself.

1. Adapted from *How to Pray for Your Children*, © 1978 by Quin Sherrer. Published by Aglow Publications, Lynwood, Wash. Used with the author's permission.

7

Becoming
Your Child's Advocate

When the ancient Greeks sent their armies to war, they sent along with the soldiers one very important person. Called a *paraclete*—literally, "someone called alongside to help"—this unarmed man went out on the battlefield to support and encourage the troops.

The paraclete, or in modern English, the "advocate," had two primary responsibilities. When the soldiers lost a battle, he would come alongside to encourage them, saying, "You have lost only a battle, not the whole war." And when the troops won a battle, he spoke to them a sobering reminder: "You have *won* only a battle, not the whole war."

When Jesus was preparing to return to His Father in heaven, He knew that we would be facing a formidable foe—Satan—on the spiritual battlefield. He also knew Satan would try to persuade us to give up in our struggle with temptation, and that we would therefore need someone to come alongside us as a helper. So Jesus told the disciples

He would send the Spirit of God to be our Paraclete, our divine Advocate (John 14:16).

Our children have the same access to the Holy Spirit we have. Yet we believe that God intends for parents as well to take the role of advocate for their children, to imitate and "make flesh" the Spirit's ministry in their young lives. After all, who has a better opportunity to listen and to advise, to support and to correct, to be available and to stand with them no matter what happens?

The parental role of advocate becomes especially important as our children reach the teen years. Adolescence brings with it physical, emotional, and spiritual transitions that can be frightening and even painful—not the least of which is awakening sexuality. Meanwhile, the whirlwind of today's secular youth culture swirls around our children, confusing them with a tempest of conflicting voices and values.

For these reasons, we're convinced that the best way to support our children in the key talk covenant is to cultivate our parental role as their advocate. More than ever before, our young people need us as their counselor and encourager, their coach and their friend.

Presence

The first aspect of a parental advocate's role is what we would call *presence*. As we said before, the core meaning of paraclete is "someone called alongside." To be an advocate, then, means first of all to be present, to be available, to be close by.

In a day when many families have both parents working outside the home, or a single parent who must make a living alone, this is a tougher challenge than ever. By now, most families seem to be realizing that the notion of "quality time," though valid in itself, can mislead us when we think of it as an appropriate substitute for *quantity* time. No doubt we need to make every moment we have with our children as "quality" as possible. But a few minutes of quality time a week just can't fill the need our children have for a close relationship with us.

We heard a pastor on a radio broadcast say recently that the average American father spends only *seventeen seconds a day* talking to his teenager. If that's true, then we must insist there's simply no way to have a quality seventeen seconds.

Some times of the day seem to lend themselves best to relationship building: the hour or so when a child first comes home from school; a relaxed dinnertime; the last few minutes of the day when a child gets into bed. But whatever hours you're able to redeem, the key is to *be there* for your child.

To be your child's advocate means to be present, to be available, and to be close by.

We suggest that you try to arrange your day so that during the times you're with your child, distractions are at a minimum. Turn off the television, radio, and stereo. Turn on the telephone answering machine, or just let the phone ring. If possible, put aside other activities for a while and talk, or else have your child join you in an activity that demands little attention so you can concentrate on each other.

Being present also means being *available*. Have you given your child permission to call you at work anytime he or she has a need? Are you willing to put down the newspaper when your son wants to talk about why girls act so "different" from guys? Can that fishing trip wait while your daughter tells you about the new boy that sits next to her in homeroom?

We heard once of a dad who was busy watching television while his son was trying desperately to engage him in conversation.

"Dad," he asked, "how do helicopters stay up in the air?"

"Hmm?" said Dad. "I don't know, son."

"Dad," his son persisted, "how do words go through a telephone line?"

"Well, uh, beats me," came the reply as Dad turned up the TV volume.

One last try. "Dad," asked the boy, "how does the walk sign make the traffic light turn red?"

"Good question," the father replied blankly and switched channels.

"Dad, I hope I'm not asking too many questions."

"Not at all, son. How will you learn if you don't ask questions?"

Such a conversation (or lack of it) makes us smile. But a child who ends up in that situation repeatedly will grow up with the conviction that Dad wasn't really there after all, even when his body was draped across the easy chair. And if the questions the child happened to be asking had to do with sex, you can be sure someone other than Dad—probably a peer at school—will end up answering them, perhaps with misinformation.

The Importance of Physical Touch

Another extremely important aspect of our presence with our children is *physical touch*. The sense of touch is

112

the first sense we acquire, while we're still in the womb. The need for physical contact begins then and continues throughout our lives.

A comforting human touch can slow down the heartbeat and reduce stress. Some studies have shown that people who are frequently touched tend to have fewer illnesses, recover more quickly from sickness, and live longer. Other research even suggests that children who receive lots of physical affection show more rapid intellectual development.

Meanwhile, the feeling of being starved for physical contact—sometimes called "skin hunger"—has decidedly unhealthy results. Have you ever seen young children who seem to misbehave just so they can be touched—even if the physical contact is a painful spanking? As James Dobson has observed, "Some children would rather be wanted for murder than not wanted at all."

Later on in the teen years, these same children may develop such a strong craving to be held that skin hunger becomes a contributor to promiscuity. They need to be touched, and sooner or later they'll find someone who'll do it.

With adolescence sometimes comes a reluctance to be touched by parents in public. If that's the case with your child, you can simply respect his or her feelings and show your affection at home. More likely, however, you may be reluctant to be physically demonstrative yourself, especially if you're a dad. Men in our culture are often trained from childhood to refrain from touching.

If that's the case, keep in mind the research indicating that parents' active affection toward their children is the most important factor in shaping their children's sexual identity. Dads who hug and kiss their sons aren't threatening their masculinity; in fact, it's the affectionate father who is most likely to encourage a normal heterosexual development in his sons. And fathers' fears about the sexual overtones of touching an adolescent daughter are usually exaggerated.

Don't forget: On certain occasions in particular, a loving touch can be critical. Be sure to show affection immediately after discipline, after family conflicts and disagreements, during times of grief, and on joyous occasions. Children, like all of us, tend to feel closest to the people they touch the most—and those people should be their parents.

Communication Skills: Listening

The second important element of an advocate relationship is *genuine communication*. And the greater part of communication is *effective listening*.

The Bible tells us we should be "quick to listen, slow to speak and slow to become angry" (James 1:19 NIV). Listening to our children says that we cherish and respect them. It also gives us a chance to understand their needs, desires, and feelings so we can advise them and stand with them in their struggles, sexual and otherwise.

Some folks say that listening has simply become a lost art. Yet we notice that when someone speaks who is highly respected or has something to say critical to our own interests, we listen carefully. We stop whatever else we're doing; we hang on every word without interruption; we study facial expressions. Listening isn't a lost art. It all depends on how much you value the one who's talking.

Could anyone on earth be more valuable to us than our precious family? Surely no one deserves our listening ear more than they do. With that insight in mind, here are a few tips for effective listening:

1. *Clear your mind of mental distractions, both inside and out*. When your child wants to talk, don't just turn off the TV; turn off the boss's comments from that morning meeting that may still be echoing in your head.

2. *Let your body language show that you're listening carefully*. Lean forward and let your face show your concern. Maintain eye contact as you listen.

   We believe that people can communicate almost as effectively with their eyes as they do with their words. Our children talk about how years ago they would often grow restless in church, squirming and whispering in the front row. As their dad preached, his eye would catch them, and that look alone was enough to settle them down.

   From the time our children were small, we've made it a practice to have them look us in the eye when responding to us. If they've done wrong, they can see in our eyes the disappointment. Our youngest son, Jonathan, reflecting back on one day when he was in the fifth grade and received correction, comments: "Mom, it wasn't the spanking I was going to get or being grounded in my room that upset me most. It was the hurt look in your eyes that I just couldn't take."

   Some say the eyes are the mirror of the soul, and we've often found that to be true—not just when we're administering correction, but also when we're listening. Maintaining eye contact with our children when they're talking to us sometimes tells us more than their words ever could.

3. *Avoid interrupting or anticipating what your child will say*. Hear your child out fully before you respond.

The Bible warns: "He who answers before listening—that is his folly and his shame" (Prov. 18:13 NIV).

4. *Listen to what your child doesn't say*. What can you hear "between the lines"? You'll never fully understand what your child is saying until you understand the words left unsaid.

5. *Listen to your child's feelings*. Sometimes you have to respond to the emotion that underlies what's being said, rather than the verbal content itself. Check your child's body language—tone of voice, facial expression, posture—for clues to what he or she is feeling at the moment. Be aware of your own feelings as well; don't let them unduly shape your perceptions of what's being said.

6. *Give regular feedback to check your comprehension*. From time to time, restate what you believe your child is saying, without evaluation, and ask your child to correct you if what you understood is incorrect.

7. *Ask questions to clarify what your child is saying*. Draw out hidden assumptions and unrecognized implications by simple queries like "Why do you think that happens?" or "What do you think will happen if that continues?"

8. *Don't judge what's said until you've heard everything*. If necessary, take some further time for consideration before responding.

9. *Answer your child's questions as thoughtfully as you can*. You may have to say, "I don't know," but even then you can show you value your child's desire for understanding by adding, "Let's see if we can find the answer together."

10. *Listen for your child's most important need at the moment.* Is he or she most in need of attention? comfort? praise? direction? a change in your behavior?

Parents who practice these guidelines for listening will encourage their children to open up again the next time they need an "advocate." Meanwhile, you'll be surprised at what you learn from them and about them.

Making Yourself Understood

The other side of communication, of course, is making yourself understood clearly. Try these guidelines for talking with your teens:

1. *Express your desires and concerns directly.* Don't drop hints or use innuendo; that only leaves your children guessing where you stand or how you feel about a matter. Young people need clear guidelines and boundaries.
2. *Share personal experiences that illustrate your points.* Include anecdotes that show your human side, your defeats as well as your victories.
3. *Don't nag or beg.* As a parent, you must come from a position of strength when you talk to your children about behaviors or attitudes that must change.
4. *Avoid "red flag words" that call for a battle.* The most common: "Always," "Never," "You're just like . . ." "Why can't you ever . . ."
5. *Express your concerns when possible with "I" statements instead of "you" statements.* Instead of accusing your child of character deficiencies ("You're irresponsi-

ble"), tell what the child's behavior does to you ("I get angry when you forget to put gas in the car and I have to do it for you").

6. *Avoid clichés.* Phrases that your child has heard a hundred times before ("Money doesn't grow on trees!") usually get tuned right out. Choose fresh ways of making your point, even if it really *is* the same point you've made over and over again.

7. *Define terms when necessary.* Are you and your child speaking with the same vocabulary? You can't always assume that's the case. For example, when you tell your son that you "plan" to take him to the ball game Saturday (with the assumption in your mind that plans sometimes fall through), does he understand the word "plan" to mean "promise" instead?

8. *Speak the truth in love* (Eph. 4:15). Not every truth can or should be spoken, and some truths must be told with great wisdom and sensitivity. But whatever we do tell our children should always be true.

Sometimes we need to "season our words with salt" (Col. 4:6). Suppose your son comes home with a haircut that looks like the barber used a buzz saw. You may be tempted to say, "I hate that stupid haircut, son! Have you lost the little bit of sense you had? You look like the freak of the block!"

Instead, try something like this: "Son, maybe you should give the barber clearer instructions about how to cut your hair. That style really doesn't do you justice. If you would like me to explain it to him next time, I'd be glad to."

The hair will grow back. But cutting words may leave wounds that fester for years to come.

Empathy

A third trait of the advocate relationship is *empathy*. The ancient paraclete on the battlefields of Greece didn't send his messages of encouragement by letter from back home. He went out with the troops to stand alongside them where they were. Though he was unarmed and couldn't fight the battle for them, he nevertheless got close enough to their struggle to be able to empathize with it.

We too need that kind of empathy with our children. We can't fight our children's battles for them, but we can learn to appreciate the difficulty of their combat. And that often requires that we put ourselves in their place or remember what it was like to be their age.

No doubt we could easily ridicule a daughter, for example, the day she comes home floating two feet off the ground with her first case of "puppy love." We could tell her it won't last and poke fun at her infatuation. But how much better an advocate we'd make if we were to recall instead what it was like the first time we ourselves got a taste of romance.

Do we remember how bright the world looked, how unimportant everything seemed next to that special someone, how every love song on the radio seemed written for us? If we can savor such memories again even for a moment, we'll be better prepared to act as an advocate for our child through the giddy days that follow a first romance—along with the inevitable crash.

> We can't fight our children's battles for them, but we can learn to appreciate the difficulty of their combat.

Boy-girl relationships are only one of the areas of concern that are likely to loom large on a teenager's emotional horizon. Adolescence typically magnifies certain issues that don't seem nearly so important later in life. If we would empathize with our children, we need to keep in mind some of the concerns that will frequently occupy their attention.

Concerns Over Physical Appearance

Teens are usually tuned in keenly not just to members of the opposite sex but to all their peers. This can lead to both an over-concern about what friends are thinking and doing as well as a perpetual anxiety over personal appearance. Thus, young people this age may feel and act as if they're continually on stage.

That means you'll need to especially affirm and compliment the physical changes taking place during adolescence. Most kids feel as if they just don't measure up to our culture's standards of beauty. Because of society's emphasis on feminine attractiveness, girls in particular may need Mom's assurance that they're pretty—and Dad may need to tease about buying his daughter a baseball bat to keep all the boys away.

Not long ago we accompanied our son Jonathan when he sang in a concert at a high school. The front row of the auditorium was filled with skinny, pimple-faced girls in braces who were passing around a magazine and giggling. It focused on the "Miss Teen USA" contest.

We caught a glimpse of the girl who held the title. Her own natural attractiveness had been enhanced by a professional makeup artist and photographer. But the girls reading the magazine probably didn't know that. All they knew was that even with the help of the best plastic surgeon, they'd probably never look like the girl in that picture.

We hope those teens had parents who were able to help them expose the subtle messages they were being fed that night. Living in a culture that constantly measures them against such unrealistic standards of appearance, they need a mom and a dad who can tell them with admiring conviction, "Honey, you're beautiful."

Other Characteristics of the Age

During the teen years, young people are also beginning to look beyond things as they are and to imagine things as they could be. Idealism may color their evaluation of life on every level (including romantic relationships) as they compare their emerging notions of a perfect world to the realities around them. Not surprisingly, young people may frequently criticize as the real world suffers by comparison to their ideal.

Accompanying such criticism may be contentiousness. As adolescents practice their developing skills of logic, they may argue just for the sake of argument or seek to know the "why" behind values they've accepted in the past without question. Empathizing with this trait may keep us from growing overly disturbed when a child seems to be questioning our moral standards—and our authority.

Finally, indecisiveness is a common characteristic of the age. Young teens in particular may agonize at times over what to wear, what to eat, what to do, and what to say. Their emerging powers of reasoning allow them to entertain so many possibilities that they may find it hard to choose among them.

If we keep in mind these tendencies of the adolescent heart and mind, we'll find it much easier to be patient with our children. At this awkward age, they desperately need the loving empathy that parents are in the best position to offer. Remember: Focus on the big picture of a child's development instead of the flaws. As someone has wisely said, love sees through a telescope, not a microscope.

Support

When you plant a little sapling, you sometimes tie it to a stake for support. Wind, rain, and snow may come, but the stake keeps the young tree from bending over or breaking beneath the pressures of the weather. So the stake remains until the tree has grown strong enough to stand straight on its own.

We like to think of parents as the stakes God has placed in the soil next to their young children. He has tied the children to their elders for a season so that they might help hold them up through life's storms until they've grown strong and straight enough to stand on their own—beautiful "trees of righteousness," as the prophet Isaiah said, "the planting of the Lord, that He might be glorified" (Isa. 61:3).

An advocate, like a close friend, supports us even when we fail—especially when we fail. Advocates speak on our behalf, plead our case, and stand at our side when we're on trial. They never bring up past failures once those failures are forgiven. Instead, they encourage us to get up and get going again. "You have lost only a battle," they remind us, "not the whole war."

That's the role of the parental advocate in the life of the child. Not only in times of failure, but in seasons of disappointment too, children need a comforter. Like stakes beside a sapling, we must hold up our children's heads and point them to the sky.

When the puppy love fails at last.... When the guy across the room in study hall doesn't even know she's alive.... When all the acne cream in the world won't cover the big pimple that showed up on his face the night of the Big Date.... At times like that, our children need to know we support them without reservation.

Correction

The ancient Greek advocate not only encouraged the troops but also brought them back to reality when they needed it. If circumstances threatened to seduce them into carelessness in the battle, he reminded them that the war was not over.

The true advocate, on the battlefield or in the home, corrects as well as supports. Advocates confront honestly but lovingly, with firmness but without condemnation. Their correction, like rain, is gentle enough to nourish the child's growth without destroying the child's roots.

Advocates also allow children the opportunity to confess their sin and repent. Then they administer cleansing discipline, give a hug, and forget it.

Some social scientists have, in fact, focused their attention on these two variables of support and correction in the parent-child relationship, and their findings support the claim that both are necessary. Such family research has identified four basic approaches to parenting.

The *authoritarian* style of child-rearing provides plenty of correction but no support. Authoritarian parents expect their children to obey without question, and their children typically rebel, run away, or live in fear.

The *permissive* style, on the other hand, offers ample support but little correction. Permissive parents make few demands; they rarely discipline and usually cave in to pressure from their children. Lacking boundaries, children in permissive homes usually feel insecure and guilty.

The *laissez-faire* style gives neither correction nor support. Children reared in this kind of home usually feel neglected, forgotten, and unloved.

Finally, the *authoritative* style of child-rearing tries to strike a healthy balance between correction and support. Authoritative parents are undoubtedly in charge, but they're also willing to listen, to answer questions, to explain their rules, and to flex when necessary.

Not surprisingly, research has shown that the fourth style—that of the authoritative parent—works best. But it's a tough challenge to maintain the authoritative approach consistently. Only with the help of the divine Advocate can we do it.

Issues as sensitive and intense as sex and romance require an extra measure of parental support as we seek to discipline our children. Lack of such support will lead only to rebellion. But at the same time, the high stakes involved in sexual issues call for unwavering standards and firm correction. Permissiveness will lead only to the tragedies of sexual mistakes, guilt, and irreversible consequences.

Support and correction—as advocates for their children, parents need to provide both.

Counsel

The Greek word *paraclete* can be translated not only as "advocate" but also as "counselor." To fulfill the role of counselor to our children, we must turn with them to the

Bible and pray for the wisdom we need. "If any of you lacks wisdom," the Scripture says, "he should ask God, who gives generously to all without finding fault, and it will be given to him" (James 1:5 NIV).

As we seek to advise our children wisely and biblically, a few particular reminders may help.

1. Sometimes the best counsel is silence and support. The older the two of us get, the more we realize that people who want to talk over their problems usually need a listening ear more than they need advice. The Bible tells us that wisdom comes from God (James 1:5), not from our own intelligence or training. So we should be sparse with our counsel, especially when it's not asked for. That's a truth we parents need to keep in mind whenever we're tempted—as we often are—to unload on our children all our great accumulation of "wisdom" so that they too can be "wise."

Renée remembers one evening walking into the room of one of our sons, who was then fourteen years old, to find him crying inconsolably. Our teen wanted to run away from home because he felt that too much of his father's time was being spent in the ministry and there was no time left for him.

Renée prayed silently that God would tell her what to say and how to counsel our son best. She knew she could give him a thousand "good reasons" why we spent so much time in ministry. Couldn't he see clearly why we were working so hard? Didn't he know it was for him? Hadn't we given our best to him and his sisters and brother? How could he demand more when we were so weary?

But no—Renée realized in that moment that all her reasons had to remain unspoken. Our son didn't need to hear Renée justify our behavior. He just needed his mother to hold him, cry with him, and after a little while, say we would try to do better. Our teen needed Renée—not her great words of "wisdom."

2. *A well-placed question can draw out the wisdom that's already in your child.* Sometimes you only need to clear away some of the confusion or distraction with wise questioning so that your child can see for him or herself the solution to a problem. In addition, children are more likely to "own" that solution and make it work when they discover it for themselves.

When Kimberli was still a young teen, Renée saw an ad for designer jeans that disturbed her. It featured a picture of a sensuous, tough-looking girl—about age fifteen—standing defiantly with her hands on her hips. Renée showed the ad to Kimberli and asked her to look at the girl and then tell what she saw.

Our daughter immediately identified the spirit of rebellion evident in the girl's eyes.

Throughout her teenage years she never forgot what she saw that day, and the realization helped her recognize that spirit when it manifested itself in her friends. We believe that the insight Kimberli gained stayed with her, at least in part, because she had discovered it for herself.

3. *Share from your experience, but recognize that your experience may be unusual.* A vivid personal anecdote with a clear lesson will more effectively make your point than a dry lecture. It will also allow your child to understand you better. But keep in mind that one person's experience doesn't necessarily apply to everyone. Avoid harping on details of "how bad it was" when you were growing up in order to make your child feel more grateful for "how good it is" now. And don't tell the same old stories again and again; they lose their punch.

The role of the parental advocate, we've seen, is multi-faceted: We must be prepared to offer our presence and support, our correction and counsel, a listening ear and an empathetic heart. With such a challenging job description, at times we may wonder whether we're doing an adequate job. But God can make up for our weaknesses, and we must realize that even our smallest efforts may mean more to our children than we know.

The story is told of a father who finally kept a promise, long overdue, to take his son fishing one Saturday morning. The day seemed rather uneventful, and that evening the dad wrote in his journal: "A totally wasted day. Nothing was accomplished."

Years later, however, when reviewing that journal entry, he chanced to compare it to the words his son had written in his diary on the same date. How had the young boy viewed that fishing trip?

"This," he wrote, "was the best day of my life."

Points to Remember

The role of an advocate for your child includes:

- Presence—being available to your child and nurturing him or her with appropriate physical affection.
- Communication skills—effective listening and making yourself clearly understood.
- Empathy—putting yourself in your child's place and recognizing the special concerns of adolescence.
- A balanced combination of support and correction.
- Counsel—sharing biblical wisdom and personal life experience.

8

Dating Goals
and Guidelines

Our son Timothy had gone out with some friends on a group date to the movie theater. He had a good idea of what kind of movies to avoid, but the title and previews of the film they'd chosen hadn't alerted him to its true contents. Soon after the movie began, Timothy realized he was watching sensual material that would pollute his mind.

Our son was in a quandary. He didn't think he could get a refund on his ticket, and he didn't want to waste the money. Worse yet, his friends weren't in agreement with him that they should leave, and he wasn't driving that night. What would he do?

Timothy got up from his seat, walked out to the lobby, and waited there alone for his friends through the rest of the film.

In some ways it would have been all too easy for a young man in Timothy's position to rationalize staying to watch the movie. If losing six dollars and sitting alone on a Saturday night didn't seem reason enough, he might have told himself that it wasn't worth alienating his friends. And the lure of the sensual material itself might have offered a strong temptation to remain.

Nevertheless, Timothy recognized the price he'd pay if he allowed the film's sexual images to impress themselves on his mind, and that he'd later reap what he'd sown. So he chose to honor God and guard his heart instead.

Your child may well encounter a similar situation—or one even more dangerous—during the dating years. With more mobility and more disposable income than ever, young people today have an unprecedented range of dating options that can be a blessing or a trap. So like most parents, you may be feeling some apprehensions about the matter.

The best protection is the kind of inner standard that motivates a young person to take a stand, even when his or her parents are not around.

How can you protect your child on dates and still allow him or her a healthy and growing measure of independence? The best protection is the kind of inner standard that motivates a young person to take a stand, even when his or her parents aren't around.

In the previous chapter we talked about how to build the kind of friendship with your children that cultivates their trust and respect. In the context of that kind of relationship, you can work with them to develop a set of personal goals and guidelines for dating to which they're firmly committed. That way, they'll have a clear inner standard to guide them when their values are challenged.

The time to establish dating goals and guidelines is *before* a child begins dating, so that there's no question from the beginning about what's appropriate and what's not. If your child has already begun dating, it's still a good time to review dating standards together in order to clear up any questions he or she may have. Either way, here are a few suggestions for the process.

Setting Goals for Dating

We noted earlier that children need some understanding of the reasons for particular moral guidelines if they're to have the strength to stand under pressure. One way to talk with them about the moral and spiritual context of dating is to explore together the *goals* they have in mind for the activity. Before they know the *how* of dating, they need to know the *why*.

Your child may be surprised to learn that dating isn't a given in every society. In some cultures young people never go out together before marriage. Young people in those cultures might wonder why Americans even date in the first place. What exactly *is* the purpose of dating?

That may sound like a strange question to some of our children, who tend to take dating for granted. But if they attempt to answer the question seriously, they can begin to get a handle on the rationale for establishing dating guidelines.

Ask your child to list the reasons why he or she wants to date. At the top of the list will probably be something like "because it's fun" or "to get to know people" or even (for older teenagers) "to find someone to marry."

Now suggest a few goals of your own. Goals like having fun and getting to know people are fine, but what about some biblical goals as well, like "to serve the other person"

131

and "to honor God"? Your child may never have thought about dating before in these spiritual terms, but to establish wholesome guidelines he or she will need to consider this aspect of the activity carefully.

The Bible tells us that we should "serve one another in love" (Gal. 5:13 NIV) and that whatever we do, we should "do it all for the glory of God" (1 Cor. 10:31 NIV). These goals are applicable to every area of our lives—dating included. So a child needs to ask: What would it mean to serve the person I'm dating and date in a way that brings glory to God rather than dishonor?

Once your child begins to identify such goals, the guidelines will begin to fall into place. If your son recognizes, for example, that he's to serve a girlfriend in love, he'll have to rule out using her for self-gratification. If your daughter knows that her dates are to honor God, then she'll have a clear reason for avoiding dishonorable places when she goes out.

Even identifying lesser goals will help your child recognize the best way to accomplish his or her purposes. For example, if one important goal is to get to know a person, then it's best to choose activities that will give a couple a chance to get better acquainted. Going on a picnic allows for ample conversation in a way that going to a movie doesn't. And even a movie provides an opportunity to get better acquainted if it's followed by a healthy "critical review" over a snack afterward.

If your child suggests inappropriate goals, you'll need to help him or her understand why they won't work. For example, looking for a marriage partner when you're sixteen will lead only to frustration, confusion, and heartache. And dating to impress the opposite sex with expensive outings in fancy places will lead only to an empty wallet!

Establishing Guidelines

Some clear standards for dating should be developed after you and your child have determined appropriate goals. The great challenge in this process is to help your child make those standards his or her *own*, held inwardly instead of imposed outwardly. You won't be on most of your child's dates to enforce the rules!

Even so, parents must take the initiative in developing dating standards. In fact, your children would probably welcome some guidelines, though they may not be willing to admit it. A survey of thirty-eight hundred undergraduates at the University of Arizona found that a third of them were either "somewhat" or "very" anxious about dating. A similar study at Indiana University discovered that half the students surveyed rated dating situations "difficult." No doubt a lack of clear boundaries in what was expected of them contributed to their sense of discomfort.

The following insights, if you go over them with your child, should help you clarify why guidelines are necessary and where they need to apply. You may even want to have your child write down each standard as you come into agreement over it. As far as possible, allow your child to craft the final form of the guideline.

No doubt you'll have to lay down some ground rules like "curfew at eleven o'clock" or "no dates alone at the beach," but even then you should allow your child's thoughts to have a fair hearing. Even if you can't reach an agreement on some point and you have to impose a decision, your child will appreciate your willingness to hear him or her out. Keep in mind that although young people appreciate boundaries, one of your own goals in this process is to help your child move more and more toward responsible *self*-control.

Remember this above all: We've found that parents who have early on established a relationship of honesty, trust, and respect with their children will have far less trouble coming to an agreement with them when it's time to set guidelines for dating.

When to Begin?

The first dating guideline to tackle is *timing*. Many dating problems—to say nothing of marriage problems—result from young people starting to date too soon. Perhaps you and your child should consider a few statistics.

According to one survey, 91 percent of girls who began dating at the age of twelve had sex before they graduated from high school. This compares to 56 percent who had dated at age thirteen; 53 percent who dated at fourteen; 40 percent who dated at fifteen; and 20 percent who dated at sixteen.

Seventy percent of ninth-grade boys with a steady girlfriend had had sex, compared to 60 percent of girls; while 52 percent of boys who dated only occasionally as freshmen had had sex, compared to 35 percent of girls.

Obviously, many young people begin dating before they're mature enough to handle it. But the question of when to begin dating remains a sensitive issue for most parents and children. If your child wants to start but you think it's too soon, that sweet preadolescent you've enjoyed so much may suddenly challenge your desire to be protective, making accusations like "You just don't trust me!" or "You don't think I'm grown-up enough!"

What *is* the right age to start dating? Actually, it's not a matter of chronological age at all; it's an issue of spiritual, moral, and emotional maturity. Before they begin dating, adolescents should be showing clear signs of responsible maturity in other areas of their lives.

Do they complete their schoolwork and give it their best? Are they faithful with their chores at home? Do they return from activities away from home on time? Do they follow family rules and parental directives? Do they show respect for others? Are they honest, especially with their parents?

The more maturity a child shows in such areas as these, the more freedom and independence he or she can be trusted with. Qualities of integrity, dependability, cooperativeness, and respect should be clearly demonstrated before children are allowed to launch out into the world of dating.

If possible, your child should know early on that you'll be watching carefully for such indications of preparedness to date. As the English philosopher John Locke once noted, "The discipline of desire is the backbone of character." Basing privilege on proven maturity in this way not only motivates children to be responsible but also teaches them that freedom and responsibility must grow together in our lives.

At the same time, however, we should note that in this, as in every area of parenting, we should extend grace to our children just as God does to us. Sadly enough, we've seen some parents who "beat" their children emotionally simply for childish or "growing up" mistakes.

For example, a child may forget about the clock while passing time away innocently enough at the mall and consequently be late coming home. If the child is genuinely sorry, how will we respond? Will we take privileges away for that display of immaturity? Or will we say, "I've been late too at times; you're generally responsible, and this one mistake won't brand you for life"?

All children will make mistakes. But we've found with our own kids that when we don't define who they are by their mistakes, they want to live up to what we believe they are.

Group and Same-Sex Activities

Younger adolescents enjoy going places with their peers and without parents, either as a group or with a good friend of the same sex. Popular activities in this category are afternoon sports events, school events, or a trip to a video arcade or shopping mall. Though some parents don't think of this as dating, it actually represents the rather natural beginnings of the dating years.

After all, most children desire to date at least in part because it allows them the chance to loosen the apron strings. If parents recognize this motivation and work along with it, group and same-sex outings can help prepare children for responsible couple dating later on.

We believe that dating should remain a group activity, or same-sex friend activity, for most of the teen years. This would include double-dating. Some exceptions might be made for special occasions like the school prom, but even then we think double dates would be better. In addition, some younger teens (fifteen to seventeen) tend to have close friends of the opposite sex without any romantic involvement; we feel that an outing with such a friend might be appropriate as long as the parent knows and approves of the companion.

Make Your Home a "Magnet"

Despite your child's push for independence, you can encourage strong and healthy ties to the rest of the family by making your home a magnet for his or her friends. Have an "open-door" policy with them, even if it means a little more noise and clutter or a little loss of privacy (and groceries).

Plan some family fun times that can include your children's friends: camping, picnics, cookie baking, selected videos and popcorn. Take up a recreational hobby they can share. Gain their respect by showing them respect, and learn to talk easily with your children's friends about serious and important matters.

Make your home a place where young people like to gather, and you'll have a great opportunity to get acquainted with your children's friends. Then you'll be better able to help them discern which crowd is a good group to go out with. Keep in mind the witty observation of poet Ogden Nash:

> One would be in less danger
> From the wiles of the stranger
> If one's own kin and kith
> Were more fun to be with.

Choosing the Right Companions

As early as elementary school, children should already be learning wise criteria for choosing their companions. Even younger children can become keen discerners of character if you instill in them over time the qualities desirable in a friend, such as integrity and maturity, kindness and thoughtfulness, diligence and dependability, good judgment and self-control—in short, biblical godliness. Once these values have been firmly established in your child, you won't have to spend much time calling the shots when they're teenagers. Their own internalized standards will allow them to evaluate their associations wisely.

In addition to character qualities, home environment can be an important factor in choosing friends. What kind of parental upbringing have they had? What's the atmosphere around their home? Is it peaceful and positive, or is it tinged with bad language, inappropriate music and television programs, or continual strife? (This is especially important if your child might be spending considerable time with friends' families.)

You can't emphasize too much to your children the importance of having friends who share their spiritual values. You can encourage their friendships with other Christians by taking an active role in your church's youth group or in other Christian ministries especially for young people.

No doubt many of their friends at school won't be Christians or come from Christian homes. But even those companions should demonstrate high moral standards if your children will be spending time with them.

Don't close your heart to your children's non-Christian friends. Instead, work with your children to win them to Christ by the love they see in your home. Invite them to church and include them in special family events where spiritual values are openly embraced. They can also take part in group dates with several Christian peers so that the positive spiritual influence is dominant.

At the same time, however, you'll want to watch closely your children's associations with non-Christians to make sure your children aren't being influenced away from their faith. This is especially the case for teens who are somewhat emotionally immature or weak in their spiritual commitment. We believe that even though our children may have friendships with non-Christians, their closest friends with whom they spend the most time—dating and otherwise—should be Christians. "Missionary dating," in which a Christian dates a non-Christian with the intent of converting him or her, rarely works and often backfires.

When our daughter Kimberli was a high school junior, she met a young man who was not a Christian but had quite a crush on her. His big desire in life at the time was to play in a rock band—hardly a candidate for a close friendship in our eyes!

Nevertheless, this young man was willing to come to any Christian meeting that would allow him to be around her, so we regularly invited him to church, youth meetings, and family dinners. We saw in him a genuine desire for Christian faith that we wanted to encourage. We knew as well that Kim had been a stable Christian for a long time, and she had strong moral standards that would not easily be compromised.

The result was that we had the privilege of introducing Kim's friend to Christ in his senior year of high school. After seven years he is still serving the Lord and has dedicated his musical talents to the kingdom of God. He's a faithful member of our church, a part of our music ministry, and best of friends with our daughter. What a mistake it would have been to close our hearts and lives to that young man simply because he'd never seen genuine Christianity lived out in a family!

Age Differences

The three years between the ages of fourteen and seventeen can make a vast difference in maturity. We regret that so many high schools now include the ninth through twelfth grades. When the ninth grade is part of junior high instead, it gives the younger teens a little more time to grow up before being thrust into the full-blown-dating, freedom-seeking mentality of juniors and seniors.

A freshman girl can look quite mature to a senior boy. But the maturity is usually physical rather than emotional. She may be thrilled by attention from an older guy, but an age gap that wide often leads to trouble.

We recommend that teens in junior high and high school date their peers—someone within two years of their own age either way. Though an older boy who's a devout Christian can be a good influence on a younger girl, even in that situation it's best that the age difference not be any greater than this.

Appropriate Places and Activities

In light of your child's goals and moral standards for dating, what are some appropriate places and activities for going out together?

As we mentioned before, dates that allow young people to maximize conversation help them toward their goal of getting to know one another better. So even though the standard date for many young people is dinner and a movie, you should encourage your child to think of some creative alternatives that will allow more interaction.

Ice- or roller-skating, horseback riding, bowling, miniature golf, theme parks, zoos, craft shows, and museums are good choices. Plays, ballets, symphonies, concerts, and related artistic programs may not allow much more conversation than movies, yet they offer a refreshing alternative. As with films, plays and concerts should be carefully screened for objectionable content.

Seasonal activities also provide plenty of opportunities for fun: hiking and mountain climbing, sailing, hayrides, Christmas caroling, marshmallow roasts, sledding, carnivals, circuses, water slides, and swimming. We recommend that young people go swimming and on hayrides only in groups.

To be avoided are places with a nightclub atmosphere that encourage sensuality, drinking, or drug abuse. This includes nightclubs, most teen clubs, dance spots, restaurants with happy hours, secular rock and jazz concerts, and even some bowling alleys. The atmosphere at some junior and senior high dances in our area—Southern California—isn't much better, though perhaps such events are more wholesome in other parts of the nation.

Dates alone in someone's home, alone at the beach while skimpily dressed, or parked in secluded spots—even in daylight—should be ruled out. And it should go without saying that films containing sexually graphic material, excessive violence, or occult or horror themes are to be avoided at all costs. As D. S. Gordon once said, "Don't let anything hang on the walls of your imagination that may not hang on the walls of your home."

What About Curfews?

Probably more parent-child conflicts over dating rules center on curfews than on any other issue. At times children may view a parent's deadline as an arbitrary limit, and they may even call it unfair or old-fashioned if their friends get to stay out later. In some metropolitan areas where crime rates continue to rise, local officials have taken the matter into their own hands by establishing legal curfews citywide. But even then, the debate may continue within families over how the rules apply.

We think parents should be open to discussing curfews. Rather than starting out with a rigid position and a defensive posture, you'll probably want to let your child tell you about the kinds of variables involved that may call for flexibility. He or she may have some important points to make about special situations that may call for exceptions or adjustments to the rules.

In general, the timing of a curfew should be governed by the degree of responsibility your child has shown. In the past, when he or she has been asked to be home by a certain time from other activities (such as afternoon visits to a friend's house), has your child proven dependable? Has he or she been careful to ask your permission to go places and called you when plans were changed? If your child is already dating, what has been his or her pattern in keeping the curfew: typically early? usually on time? consistently late with a variety of excuses?

We'd suggest earlier deadlines for children who haven't yet demonstrated a responsible attitude in this regard. The time limit can be extended as the child proves him or herself to be more responsible.

In general, we've found these five rules helpful with our own children:

1. Establish clearly a time to be home.
2. Be willing to make exceptions for special nights. For example, a church outing at the beach or a pizza party in the home of a family you know and respect may last beyond this time. Or a particular movie may last

three hours, and the only way to meet the normal curfew would be to leave in the middle of the film.

3. Children must always call if they need to make an exception to the curfew and no prior arrangements were made for extended hours.

4. All dates should be planned. The plans should then be reported to parents and followed as closely as possible. If plans change, a phone call home can settle any questions.

5. If children cooperate with the above rules and respect the general curfew by staying close to it—that is, they always come home within half an hour of the deadline and aren't consistently late—then it's not necessary to be rigid. Rigidity can lead to much unnecessary conflict and unhappiness.

For example, if the curfew is 11:00 and your child walks in at 11:05, it's a bit unreasonable to be angry, making accusations and doling out restrictions. Consider the particular circumstances, and remember that even we who are parents sometimes misjudge the heaviness of freeway traffic or other factors that are out of our control. Allowing for some flexibility, if the child doesn't take advantage of it, builds in your child more of a sense of being trusted and a desire to maintain that trust.

Petting

Even young people who understand clearly that sexual intercourse outside of marriage is wrong may have questions about what kind of physical activity is "allowed." With regard to petting, the almost-inevitable question of the teen years is "How far is too far?" We believe that this issue is so important it deserves a separate chapter.

Points to Remember

- To clarify dating guidelines for your child, you should first help him or her clarify goals for dating.
- The time to begin dating depends not on a child's chronological age, but on the evidence he or she has shown of responsible maturity in other areas of life.
- For most of the teen years, dating should primarily be double-dating, dating in groups, or activities with friends of the same sex.
- Make your home a magnet for your child's friends, where they enjoy spending time with your family.
- Help your child learn wise criteria for choosing friends.
- Establish clear ground rules for curfews and appropriate places and activities for dating.

9

How Far Is "Too Far"?

We know a young man who used to pray, "Lord, please take away from me this attraction to the opposite sex." But the Lord had to let him know that He couldn't answer such a prayer because it's *healthy* to have that attraction.

Today when we talk to young people about sexual temptation, we like to emphasize that they have desires of this kind not because there's something wrong with them, but because there's something *right* with them. They've been "wired" that way by a Creator who has designed them to experience sexual pleasure in marriage. But if they fail to understand the "circuitry" of that biological wiring, they can get into trouble.

A Momentum Not Easily Stopped

When young people ask a question like "How far is too far?" they usually have at least two misconceptions in mind about how their sexuality is designed. The first misconception is that sexual foreplay (petting), which arouses the body for intercourse, can be easily stopped at any point once it's begun.

Try offering this comparison to your child as you talk about the dangers of petting: If you drive down a neighborhood street at eighty miles an hour and a child runs out in front of you, you'll probably hit the child. No matter how hard you press down the brake or how sincere your intention of stopping, the outcome is nearly inevitable because your tragic choice was already made earlier—when you chose to go that speed in a residential area.

God not only gives us grace to control ourselves; He gives us wisdom about how to do it as well.

We like to tell young people that sexual temptation is much like that drive through a neighborhood. If a couple doesn't draw the line early on so that they don't get sexually aroused in the first place, they'll reach a point where it's nearly impossible to stop. Establishing the rules ahead of time, with both parties in agreement, is critical for avoiding tragic results.

The Scriptures make us a beautiful promise with regard to sexual temptation (and temptation of all kinds):

> No temptation has seized you except what is common to man. And God is faithful; he will not let you be tempted beyond what you can bear. But when you are tempted, he will also provide a way out so that you can stand up under it.
>
> 1 Corinthians 10:13 NIV

Nevertheless, if we go hunting for the temptation and then expect God to guard us from it, we'll get burned. In the same passage, it says: "So, if you think you are standing firm, be careful that you don't fall!" (v. 12). God not only gives us grace to control ourselves; He gives us wisdom about how to do it as well.

For that reason, we believe petting—the caressing of another person in sexual play—should be off limits outside of marriage. It's the spark that gets the fire burning, often till it becomes a fire out of control. And even when one member of the couple is unwilling to have intercourse, that's still no guarantee it won't happen; the rising statistics on date rape reflect that reality.

French Kissing, Sensual Imagery, and Pornography

Though some people assume that kissing in any form should be all right for singles, French kissing has the potential to cause deep sexual arousal. The respected sex therapists Doctors Masters and Johnson observed that French kissing is, in fact, a simulation of sexual intercourse, in which the tongue functions like the penis and the mouth like the vagina, with a thrusting in and out that imitates coitus (genital intercourse). So to engage in French kissing is to be asking for temptation and moral failure.

Sometimes the wildfire is lit even before a couple comes in contact with each other. Young men especially must guard their eyes in a culture where so much visually sensuous material is constantly presented. If teenagers watch a sex scene on television, at a movie, or read about one in a magazine, they may well feel a growing desire to act out that scene on a date.

Convicted rapist and serial murderer Ted Bundy, commenting on his past in an interview just before he died in

147

the electric chair, admitted that he got started on the road of sexual crime by reading pornography. And if he'd had available what teens have today on magazine racks and video store shelves, he may well have done much worse, much sooner.

An Artificial Line

The second misconception we find among young people is the notion that coitus—that is, penetration of the female's vagina by the male's penis, usually resulting in orgasm for one or both—is sex in the strict sense of the word, and other kinds of sexual activity are somehow less dangerous or not as immoral. This way of thinking says that even if the Bible forbids sex outside of marriage, it's talking only about coitus, leaving petting, mutual masturbation, oral intercourse, and anal intercourse as acceptable options for unmarried couples.

Some young people who don't "go all the way" (in itself a misleading phrase) still think it's all right to engage in a number of other sexual behaviors such as giving "hickeys" (temporary red marks produced by intense sucking and biting), lying together naked without intercourse, or fondling of genitals. But we find it hard to see how any moral distinction can be maintained between those kinds of activities and coitus. As author John White once asked:

> Is there any moral difference between two naked people in bed petting to orgasm and another two having intercourse? Is the one act a fraction of an ounce less sinful than the other? Is it perhaps more righteous to pet with clothes on? If so, which is worse, to pet with clothes off or

to have intercourse with clothes on? (John White, *Eros
Defiled*, as quoted by Barry Wood, *Questions Teenagers Ask
About Dating and Sex*, Old Tappan, New Jersey: Fleming
H. Revell, 1981, p. 84.)

The point is this: Sexual intercourse and other forms
of sexual activity really represent the same moral issue.
They all have an impact on the human soul with sobering
consequences, resulting in powerful feelings of bonding
and—outside of marriage—guilt, shame, and damaged
self-esteem.

Some people argue that sexual acts without the penis's
penetration of the vagina are more acceptable because the
female's virginity is left intact. No doubt a technical diction-
ary definition of a "virgin" is "a person who has not had
sexual intercourse, especially a girl or a woman." But that
technicality has little meaning when a couple has engaged
in mutual masturbation or oral or anal sex.

From a psychological or spiritual point of view, what's the
difference? If we engage in these types of activities outside
of marriage, we're still sinning in that we're dishonoring
our bodies, damaging our emotions, and corrupting our
thoughts. During other kinds of sex, in essence, sexual intercourse is committed in our heart (see Matt. 5:27).

Defrauding a Partner

The Bible speaks of these other kinds of sexual activities
as a couple's *defrauding* of each other. To *defraud* a person
sexually is to arouse sensual desires in that person that cannot be *righteously* satisfied. The Bible warns us to avoid this
behavior:

For this is the will of God, your sanctification; that is, that you abstain from sexual immorality; that each of you know how to possess his own vessel in sanctification and honor, not in lustful passion, like the Gentiles who do not know God; and that no man transgress and defraud his brother in the matter because the Lord is the avenger in all these things, just as we told you before and solemnly warned you. For God has not called us for the purpose of impurity, but in sanctification.

1 Thessalonians 4:3–7 NASB

So sexual purity doesn't mean doing everything except genital intercourse. It represents an intent to "possess our own vessels"—that is, our bodies—in holiness and honor.

The Danger of STDs

Your child needs to know yet another important reason not to engage in petting, mutual masturbation, or oral and anal sex: These activities can lead to the transmission of STDs.

Genital herpes, a viral infection that causes painful sores in the genital area and sometimes blisters in the mouth, can be transmitted by oral and anal sex, kissing, and touching of active sores. In addition to the sores, symptoms include swollen glands, muscle aches, fever, and pain on urination. Often the sufferers cannot sit or walk.

These symptoms last four to six weeks, but afterward the virus doesn't go away. Once infected, a patient is infected for life, with periodic recurrences of symptoms. The disease can be transmitted even when no symptoms occur.

If an infected woman gives birth without a Cesarean section, there is a possible one in two chance they will pass the disease along to the child, who may as a result die or be severely disabled. No cure is known for herpes.

Chlamydia trachomatis, the most common STD in women, can be contracted through contact with the genitals of an infected person and even during oral sex. Men can contract the disease as well, but they rarely have any observable symptoms. Without treatment, chlamydia may damage the cells of the cervix and promote cervical cancer.

The virus that causes AIDS can also be transmitted through any sexual activity that includes the transfer of semen or blood. This would include oral sex and anal sex. We should note in particular that because anal sex typically results in breakage of the lining of the anus, it poses the greatest of all sexual risks for transmission of AIDS and other STDs.

As we mentioned in an earlier chapter, there are no known cases of the AIDS virus being transmitted by French kissing, but the possibility of such transmission exists. In addition, gonorrhea can be passed on by French kissing if one of the partners has an oral infection, which often occurs through oral sex. And even syphilis can be transmitted by petting or French kissing if the infected partner has a cut or abrasion in the mouth.

With all these insights in mind, your child should be able to understand the spiritual, emotional, and physical dangers of sexual activity outside of coitus. We suggest that he or she try asking a different question than "How far is too far?" It is more helpful and accurate to ask, "Would God be pleased or disappointed by what I'm thinking about doing?"

Points to Remember

- Two misconceptions are common among young people:

1. The false notion that sexual foreplay can easily be stopped once it's begun.
2. The idea that sexual activities other than coitus are somehow less immoral or less dangerous.

- The Bible insists that single people who engage in non-coital sex are sinning by defrauding each other.
- STDs can be transmitted through non-coital sex.

10

Wisdom, the Context

The British have an old joke they like to tell whenever an American is around. Once upon a time, they say, the head groundskeeper for the White House went to visit the chief gardener at Buckingham Palace in London. After surveying the magnificent lawn at the palace, the American asked: "How do you get your lawn to look like that? The grass at the White House is not nearly so beautiful."

"Well," said the palace gardener, "first you seed it well."

"Yes," said the American. "We do that too."

"Then," said the Englishman, "you fertilize it well."

"Yes," the White House groundskeeper replied. "We certainly do that."

"Then," said the Englishman, "you water it well."

"Of course," said the American. "So do we."

"Then," said the palace gardener, smiling triumphantly, "you repeat the process for five hundred years."

In presenting the idea of a key talk, we feel a bit like the gardener at Buckingham Palace. We can describe step by step the particular strategy we've used to help our children remain sexually pure. But we must also recognize that this strategy is only one part of a larger, long-term approach to parenting—a process of seeding, fertilizing, and watering repeatedly over the years—that cultivates a beautiful character in our children.

This book focuses on the simple idea of a key talk and a few immediately related issues; it's not intended as a comprehensive guide to parenting. But we want to emphasize our awareness that there are no quick, simple formulas for parents seeking to raise children with strong moral standards. Without the broader context of a healthy atmosphere at home, the key talk could easily become just another gimmick.

There are larger foundations on which the key talk must rest. . . . We use the acronym WISDOM: Worth, Integrity, Security, Destiny, Ownership, Marital Commitment.

In light of that reality, we want to take two chapters simply to discuss some of the larger issues parents face in child-rearing. No doubt we have only space here to note briefly a few critical qualities parents need to cultivate in their family life. But we don't want to offer you a book on the key talk without at least mentioning some of the larger foundations on which an effective key talk rests.

To help you remember the following points, we've used the acronym WISDOM. In this context, that word stands for worth, integrity, security, destiny, ownership, and marital commitment—all essential to the growth of a child who is healthy in body, soul, and spirit. The first three elements will be discussed in this chapter, and the last three in chapter 11.

Worth

No doubt every parent can remember how their young children would call out from the swings on the playground: "Watch me, Mommy! Look, Daddy! See how high I can go!" Then those little ones would pump their legs with all their might, just to make their parents proud.

Do our children ever really grow out of that need for our approval and applause? Probably not. No one on earth can affirm a child the way a parent can. Especially when they're younger, they tend to just accept our evaluation of them—no matter how flawed our perspective might be.

For that reason, our children's image of themselves is largely borrowed from us and then built upon in later years as they try to find a place of value and acceptance in the world. Our challenge, then, is to build in them a strong sense of self-esteem. Why is a sense of personal worth so critical? The way we view ourselves inevitably affects every aspect of our lives. People who perceive themselves as valuable tend to think, feel, and behave in more positive, constructive ways than those whose self-esteem is weak.

In the life of a child, self-esteem is the world's most powerful antidote to peer pressure. If a child doesn't think very highly of him or herself, then the desire to please peers in order to gain some form of acceptance will be a strong motivator in behavior. The fear of ridicule or rejection by friends will carry considerable weight.

This is especially true in youthful friendships with the opposite sex. Insecurity about their own worth or importance can push children to look for identity and value in prematurely close relationships with a boyfriend or girlfriend. The pressure to express this desire sexually can be nearly overwhelming.

A Sense of Importance

How do we build a sense of personal worth in our children? To do that we need to recognize that self-esteem has three major building blocks. The first of these is *a sense of importance*.

One way to help our children feel worthwhile is to teach them who they are in Christ. A solid identity as a beloved child of God for whom Christ died—and within whom Christ lives—provides the basis for true, biblical self-esteem in a young person.

We've tried to teach our children from their earliest days that God cherishes them. They've heard us say often that God took great delight in creating them—that He personally wove together their traits while they were still in the womb—and that they are by no means an accident. Even now, they know, God is so interested in every detail of their lives that the very hairs on their heads are numbered (Ps. 139:14–15; Matt. 10:30).

The knowledge that they're worth so much to God strengthens our children during the times when they might otherwise be tempted to give themselves away to the world. Realizing that their bodies are holy masterpieces made by God, they can recognize that sex outside of marriage would violate such holiness. So like Joseph when he was tempted by Potiphar's wife, they're able to refuse sin's invitation, because they refuse to "sin against God" (Gen. 39:9).

A second key to our children's sense of worth is our consistent affirmation of *who they are* as distinct from *what they do*. Sometimes we need to take a minute just to show our children our approval of them apart from anything they may have accomplished. We need to let them know from time to time that we take delight in them just as they are.

Our second daughter, Anna, could hardly have been more different from our first daughter, Kimberli. In school Kim was a straight-A overachiever. Anna, on the other hand, was not under the pressure of making good grades.

Anna, in the second grade, thought it was wonderful when the teacher marked through so many answers on her papers with a big red X. After all, red was her favorite color! We'll never forget the paper on which Anna had written across the top, "Dear teacher, I love you. I am your pet." Just below her comment the teacher replied: "I love you too, Anna—F."

Anna, you see, was just happy about life. She couldn't care less about grades, but her happiness brought joy to all those around her. So we had to come to grips with the difference between our two daughters and recognize that our appreciation for who Anna was didn't depend on her performance in school. She was who she was, and we delighted in her just as we delighted in her sister.

Late one day Renée watched Anna, who was twelve, sitting on a curb across the street, deep in thought as she was writing something. Often she would pause and look up to the darkening sky as she searched for just the right word. Finally she came into the house, showered Renée with her usual hugs and kisses, and handed her this poem:

> You are the blossoms in the spring,
> Snow in the winter.
> You are the breeze on a summer night—
> the joy of the winter.
> You are the prize of my father,
>   the jewel of my life,
>   my mother.
> You bring hope and understanding

> when there
> is none there.
> This is my poem
> of you—Mother Dear!
> Love, Anna

Today Anna is a sensitive, mature, and godly young woman. The good grades finally came. But much more importantly, the wonderful personal qualities we love so much have never faded.

A third contributor to our children's sense of importance is our *words of love, acceptance, and confidence*. "Death and

"I love you. I believe in you. I trust you. I respect you." These are words of life.

life," the Bible says, "are in the power of the tongue" (Prov. 18:21 NASB). We can build an atmosphere of affirmation in our homes by what we say to and about our children. "I love you. I believe in you. I trust you. I respect you." These are words of life.

A fourth key in this area is one we mentioned before: *physical affection*. When children lack proper affection, they feel rejected and unwanted. And because they need that affection so much, they'll go looking for it somewhere else—usually in a sexual relationship.

A Sense of Belonging

The second major building block of self-worth is *a sense of belonging*. To feel valuable, children need a confident awareness that they have a special *place* in the world where they fit. That sense of place helps provide them with an identity, a clearer sense of who they are.

Children need to be able to say, "I belong here. This is my family. This is my home. This is my room. These are my toys, my clothes."

To cultivate this sense of belonging, children need a clear picture of what it is they belong to. That means we should do all we can to clarify and strengthen our family's identity. Here are some suggestions:

- Talk together about what makes your family distinctive. Focus especially on the values you hold as a family that may set you off from our culture as a whole. When your family's values are challenged by difficult circumstances or the opposition of those who think differently, rally together and provide mutual support.

- Explore your family tree. If you have a family crest, talk about what it symbolizes and display it. Interview older relatives in your extended family and record an oral history of your "clan." Find out the special events and circumstances that have contributed to making your family what it is today.

- Stress family unity by engaging in recreational activities everyone can take part in. Resist our society's tendency to separate families into age categories for instruction and service.

- Celebrate your family. Take family snapshots frequently, then display them liberally. Make matching buttons or T-shirts that symbolize your family's unity and spirit. Turn every birthday, anniversary, or other special occasion into an opportunity to express your appreciation for one another.

- Reminisce often as a family. Recall family outings, comical anecdotes, warm memories, and crises overcome together.

- Keep in touch with relatives through letters, phone calls, visits, and family reunions. Put up a bulletin board where you display photos, letters, and news clippings about your extended family.
- Build family traditions that affirm your family's values; involve every family member and celebrate your relationships.

A Sense of Ability

The third major building block of self-esteem is *a sense of ability*. Children need to know that they can make a contribution to the world. To value themselves, they must have a sense of competence in certain capabilities that allow them to make a difference in the lives of others.

We've already said that children need to know they're valued *apart* from their accomplishments. But their accomplishments shouldn't be ignored. All people desire to achieve something of importance in their lives, to show a worthwhile return on the investment of their time and energies. This desire to be competent begins in childhood, and as parents we need to help our children satisfy it.

Our children's sense of ability can be encouraged in small ways, like displaying our children's artwork proudly in our home. We also bolster their confidence in their own abilities when we attend their sports events or concerts. And we strengthen their self-image when we encourage them to "hang in there" during a challenging athletic season, knowing that in the end they'll feel better about themselves if they didn't quit when the going got tough.

Above all, however, we encourage our children to grow confident in their ability to remain content in the midst of challenges when we emphasize the truth of the apostle Paul's words: "I can do all things through Him who strengthens me" (Phil. 4:13 NASB). We become our children's most effective cheerleaders with this promise: "You can do *anything* in Christ—there's never anything impossible with Him!"

In all these ways, then, we can cultivate our children's self-esteem. In the world they face today, they'll certainly need it. As author Alvin Price once said, "Parents need to fill a child's bucket of self-esteem so high that the rest of the world can't poke enough holes in it to drain it dry."

When Richard was young, he had ample reason in the eyes of the world to suffer from low self-esteem. He was skinny and wore thick glasses—the kind that earned him all kinds of ugly nicknames from schoolmates. Worse yet, he struggled with bed-wetting up until his high school years. He was the victim of parental divorce at the age of ten, which robbed him of his father's physical, emotional, and financial support.

Nevertheless, Richard was assured of his mother's and grandmother's love, and because of them, he was confident of God's love as well. They persuaded him that he was important, that he belonged, and that he had a contribution to make. So what other people thought about him didn't matter so much.

Richard grew up in a tough neighborhood where peer pressure was formidable. The young men around him often pressed him to engage in sex like the rest of them were doing. But that strong sense of personal worth his family had instilled in him gave him the strength to say no.

The apostle Paul said that "the love of Christ constraineth us" (2 Cor. 5:14). External controls are of only limited value. But when our children know without a doubt that they're loved—by God and by their parents—that love provides the inner restraint they need to stay pure.

Integrity

The core meaning of the word *integrity* is *wholeness* or *consistency*. To have integrity is to be well "integrated"—that is, what we say and what we do should be in harmony and all of one piece.

To "train up a child in the way he should go" (Prov. 22:6), we have to go that way ourselves. Levi Miller once wrote: "You can punish any child you have the right and strength to punish. But you can discipline only those children who choose to be your disciples; that is, who follow you, pattern after you, love and respect you."

In no season of life is that statement more true than in adolescence. During those years, youthful ideals often make hypocrisy look like the unforgivable sin. So not even our most persuasive lecture about purity could ever have as much impact as a consistent example of godliness in our own lives.

The faulty but prevailing notions in our culture about sex and romance must be overcome by our children if they're to develop an accurate and healthy view of love and marriage. Most often the mass media images tell them that love is a sentimental emotion attached to strong sexual feelings that must not be denied.

There's probably only one way that such powerful media illusions can be stripped of their credibility: They must be exposed by comparison to the reality of a healthy model of love and sexuality. If our children can see concrete examples of a faithful and satisfying marital relationship, they'll more easily see our society's lie for what it is.

Parents are obviously in the best position to offer their children a healthy model that can be observed closely day in and day out. In fact, children will tend to accept as the norm the patterns of male-female relationships they see lived out at home. That places an enormous responsibility on us parents, but it also gives us an unparalleled opportunity to inoculate children against the distorted and artificial models of love and sexuality they see in the movies, on TV, and elsewhere.

If we want our children to love something, we must truly love it ourselves. Do we truly love holiness? Have we genuinely given ourselves to a standard of sexual purity before God? Can our children see in our marriage a clear example, however imperfect, of faithful love?

In addition, our adult friendships speak volumes to our children about the kind of associations that are godly. Are there other families we know who can serve as role models for our children? Can we point to other couples close to us and say, "There's another example of two people who know how to love each other for a lifetime"?

No doubt even the best of us have our weaknesses and flaws. But even when we fail, we can model the right behavior to our children by admitting to them our failure. Integrity isn't so much a perfect consistency as it is a persistent willingness to let God make us consistent.

Security

One study[1] has shown that children whose families rely upon food stamps for survival or who have an unemployed parent are more likely than other children to engage in dangerous behavior. They're three times as likely to feel the pressure to take drugs, twice as likely to feel pressure to disobey authority, four times as likely to feel pressure to join a gang, and six times as likely to feel pressure to have sex.

What's the message here? No doubt a number of variables are at work in these statistics. But we believe the figures suggest that insecurity weakens a child's resistance to temptation. Young people who must live under financially uncertain circumstances appear more susceptible to the negative pressures of society than their more secure peers.

Yet financial uncertainty is only one type of insecurity. Some children continually worry that their family might break up. Their fears are fed by their parents' open bickering or perhaps even shouted threats about leaving.

Other young people simply sense an uneasiness at home, an undercurrent of instability from a lack of trust in their family relationships. Their parents tend to be undependable in their commitments, unpredictable in their moods, and inconsistent in their discipline. They rarely share what they're thinking and feeling. So the children are never quite certain where they stand at home.

It takes very little wisdom to conclude that children like these, for whom home is an insecure place, will go looking for a haven somewhere else. As they search, they'll be vulnerable to the ungodly pressures they encounter, whether their insecurity is financial or otherwise. And if the seemingly "safest" place they can find is in the arms of a boyfriend or girlfriend, sex will easily be mistaken for security.

Home should be the safest place your children know— not just physically and financially, but emotionally as well. Young people need parents who can trust and be trusted, who can keep a confidence and forgive a failure. They need stable adults who can control their tempers and work out solutions to problems calmly. They need a home with at least a few traditions and some dependable structure to help make sense out of the chaos of modern life.

In short, children need security—some comfortable rhythms, a sense of roots, and even a little routine.

Points to Remember

The key talk is most effective when placed in a context of "WISDOM," which includes these elements:

- Worth—Parents should help the child develop adequate self-esteem—which includes a sense of importance, of belonging, and of making a contribution to the world.
- Integrity—What parents do should be in harmony with what they say.
- Security—Home should be a safe place physically and emotionally.

1. "Girl Scouts survey on the beliefs and moral values of America's children," Fieldwork: Fall, 1989, Executive Summary.

11

Wisdom, Part 2

Imagine that right in the middle of the Boston marathon, an official came out to the runners with an announcement over a loudspeaker.

"Your attention, please! We must inform you that the finish line for this race has now been dismantled, and the route markers taken away. You no longer have a particular destination nor a clearly marked path to get there. Nevertheless, we encourage you just to choose any street and keep running, even though it will be impossible to declare a winner. Good luck and have fun!"

Under those conditions, who would be foolish enough to keep running the race? In fact, how could you even call it a race?

Sadly enough, we believe that many young people today are in a situation much like that race without a finish line. As they consider what they want to do with their lives, they realize that they're at the starting block, or perhaps even some distance into the run—yet they haven't a clue about where they're going or how they'll get there. Is it any wonder, then, that they've lost the motivation to run?

Many folks today have *goals* but no *purpose* in life. What's the difference? A goal is a *what*; a purpose is a *why*.

We recently heard a popular Christian speaker repeat a comment his daughter made while in law school. "Dad," she observed, "I listen to countless conversations among my fellow law students as they talk about what they're doing. And you know what's disturbing? Though they all talk about what's *legal*, never once have I heard anyone talk about *justice*."

That's the difference between a goal and a purpose. Those students may have the potential for a brilliant career in law. But if they never think beyond the goal of winning legal cases to the over-arching purpose of achieving justice, their work will be hollow and even misdirected. Failing to serve justice, they'll most likely end up serving themselves.

Whether our children turn out to be lawyers, janitors, or some job title not yet invented, they need a personal *destiny*. They need to know where they're headed and why. If they don't have a destination in life to draw them on and keep them on the right path, they'll either give up the race or end up somewhere they'd rather not be.

As parents, we may not be in a position to tell our children precisely what their destiny is. But we can certainly cultivate in them from an early age the awareness that God has created them for a special purpose that no one else can fulfill. Children need a destination if they are to have hope. And hope, the Bible tells us, can motivate them to keep themselves pure (see 1 John 3:3).

Destiny

When we look at our children, what do we see? Sadly enough, some parents view their children as a burden, counting the years until the little ones will grow up to become independent. Others see them as such an inconvenience that they kill the baby in the womb before they even have a chance to see the light of day. To a great extent, this is a generation without hope.

When Moses was born a slave in ancient Egypt, Pharaoh had decreed that all the newborn boys of the Hebrews should be killed. Talk about an "inconvenience"! To keep the child was more than a strain on the budget of a slave family. Disobeying Pharaoh to protect the child could have meant death.

Nevertheless, the Bible tells us, Moses' mother didn't see her little boy as a burden. Instead, "she saw . . . that he was a goodly child" and risked her life to save him (Exod. 2:2). We believe that she saw Moses through the eyes of faith, trusting in God that her little infant had the potential for greatness.

Moses' mother probably had little idea that her son would become the great liberator of his people from Egyptian bondage, nor that he would one day speak to the Lord "face to face" like a close friend (Deut. 34:10). But she didn't have to know the specifics. She simply knew that in God's eyes, as in her own, Moses was "a goodly child."

In such a wicked day, when Satan is crushing the lives of young people on every side— God, help us see the seed of greatness in our beautiful children!

God, grant us eyes like that mother had! In such a wicked day, when Satan is crushing the lives of young people on every side—God, help us see the seed of greatness in our beautiful children! If we see it, believe it, proclaim it, and nurture it in the soil of our children's hearts, that seed of greatness will sprout and grow far beyond what we might imagine.

Moses' mother believed that her son's life would be spared. So she made preparation for his future by building a little ark, setting him afloat in the Nile, and sending his sister Miriam to watch him (Exod. 2:3–4). Do we also believe that our "goodly" children will be spared from the suicide, drugs, sexual sins, and other devastation Satan has planned for them? Do we believe it firmly enough to plan for their future and point them toward the purposes of God for their lives?

Parents play a critical role in pointing their children toward their destiny for two reasons. First, children are profoundly shaped by the expectations of their parents. If Dad and Mom say they can be a great man or woman of God, they're likely to agree.

Second, parents are in a position to instill hope in young people long before anyone else has a major chance to influence them. The sooner children are aware that God has plans for them, the sooner they can begin moving toward His purposes.

In fact, the Bible shows us that many great men and women of God were called to their destiny at a young age. Samuel was a little boy when God first spoke to him. David was a youth when he was anointed king. Jeremiah was probably a teenager when God called him to prophesy, and Mary was almost certainly a young adolescent when Gabriel announced to her that she would bear the Savior of the world.

Evidently, to fulfill the purposes God had for these men and women, He had to apprehend them early in life. If knowledge of their calling had been delayed until adulthood, it might have been too late. By then they might have fallen into sin that could frustrate or even forestall the plan of God for their lives.

The same may be true of our children as well. Even if they can't yet know the details of God's purpose for them, we nevertheless need to communicate the seriousness of the call on their lives as early as possible. If they are to reach the finish line of God's destination, then they must stay on track even now.

Only if our children begin early to "throw off everything that hinders and the sin that so easily entangles" can they be assured that they will "run with perseverance the race marked out" for them (Heb. 12:1 NIV). In matters of sexual purity especially, one failure alone could wreck a life, with repercussions that could last for generations.

A revivalist once reported on the results of an evangelistic meeting with this observation: "Two and a half souls were saved."

"Do you mean two adults and one child?" someone asked.

"No," came the firm reply. "Two children and one adult. The adult only has half his years left to serve the Lord, but each of the children still has a whole lifetime."

Our children, too, still have a whole life to accomplish the purposes of God. So we must issue them a challenge: If God had wanted Moses or Peter for this generation, He would have placed Moses or Peter in our time. But instead, God arranged for *you* to be born for such a time as this. He needs *you* for this generation. You have a special assignment from God, a part to play in His kingdom on the earth. What great thing does God want to accomplish through you?

With this conviction, are we in danger of raising our children's expectations too high? We don't believe that's possible. "Never tell a young person that anything cannot be done," wrote John Andrew Holmes. "God may have been

171

waiting for centuries for somebody ignorant enough of the impossible to do that very thing."

Ownership

A friend of ours remembers how when he was young, a grade school teacher once asked his class to "vote" on the two candidates in an upcoming presidential election. She counted the show of hands for each side, and though the youngsters obviously couldn't cast their votes in the real contest, she nevertheless seemed pleased that the majority backed the candidate of her choice. Later on, our friend overheard her confiding to another teacher: "I like to find out how the kids would vote, because you can be sure that's how their parents will vote."

She was probably right. But the results would have been quite different if that teacher had gone to the nearby high school to ask for a vote. She could no longer have assumed that the students' choices were reflecting those of their parents. In fact, she might well have found many who were intentionally voting the *opposite* of how they knew their parents would vote. By that age, many of the young people would have been expressing their own, often passionate, opinions.

Why the difference? Typically, young children uncritically accept their parents' values. In matters of politics, faith, and morals especially, if Mom and Dad say it's so, then it must be so.

But healthy adolescents must sooner or later outgrow that way of discerning right from wrong and truth from error. To become responsible adults, they must mature to the place where the values they cherish aren't borrowed from parents or others, but rather belong to them personally. Children must come to *own* their faith and their moral standards.

The purpose of parental discipline in our children's lives should be to help them make that transition into ownership of their values. We must cultivate in them a steady progression from external control to inner restraint, from doing things because Mom and Dad say so to doing things because it's *right* to do them.

Nowhere is this transition more important than in the area of sexual morality. We can't be with our children every moment, and our lectures alone won't do much to slow things down in the backseat of a car on Saturday night. But a strong personal conviction that sex should be reserved for marriage will accompany our children wherever they go, providing them an inner "rock" on which they can take a stand.

How do we encourage this process? Most young people will initiate the change on their own, questioning their standards and giving some thought to alternative values. So it's up to the parents to recognize that the transition is necessary and then to respond to their children's thinking with respect. Here are a few brief tips:

- Don't view your child's challenge of your values as an assault on your authority or integrity. The real question behind that challenge is not "Who are you to make the rules?" but rather "How can you convince me that these standards are valid?"
- Don't ridicule your child's attempts at formulating new positions, even if they seem foolish. Show respect for your child's integrity in trying to avoid hypocrisy and find genuine faith.
- Together with your child, prayerfully search the Scriptures for insights into personal values and standards.

173

- Know clearly what you believe yourself. Then, when you're challenged, patiently explain as clearly as possible the reasons you take the position you do. Are your reasons based on the Scriptures? common sense? experience?

- When possible, challenge your child's misdirected lines of thinking by gentle questioning rather than blunt attack. The ancient "Socratic method"—in which teachers help students discover truth for themselves by asking questions that make them think logically—is still an excellent approach to learning. And a position young people arrive at by this method is one they are much more likely to "own," since they've discovered it themselves.

- When your child makes a good choice, affirm it with praise. Then help your child clarify what kind of values and reasoning went into making the decision.

- When your child makes a bad choice, help him or her explore the reasons. What kind of faulty values or reasoning might have contributed to the decision? Understanding the context of the mistake may help your child avoid making it again.

We once read about a Christian mother who was shocked to find a copy of *Playboy* under her son's mattress. The father's response was calm. He sat down with the boy for a talk, opening with a comment something like this: "I understand you've been trying to catch up on your sex education by looking at *Playboy*."

The dad didn't condemn his son or try to manipulate him with a sense of guilt. Instead, he said patiently, "I'd like to tell you the reasons I decided not to read magazines like that."

Then he went on to explain the values and the reasoning that stood behind his own standards in that area.

The young man wasn't put on the defensive with ridicule or condemnation. So he was free to listen and appreciate why his father had taken a certain stand. They even went on to discuss how his father dealt with sexual temptation.

Can you imagine a better way to help a child grow into a personal ownership of biblical values?

When Richard was five years old, his mother taught him a little poem that illustrates the importance of allowing our children to make their own spiritual commitments:

> Said the laddie to the father
> on one bright and sunny day,
> May I give my heart to Jesus,
> let Him wash my sin away?
> No, my son, you are too little;
> wait until you older grow.
> Older ones are true to need Him;
> little ones are safe, you know.
> Said the father to the laddie
> as a storm was coming on—
> are the sheep all safely sheltered
> safe within the fold, my son?
> All the big ones are, my father,
> but the little ones, I let them go,
> for I did not think it mattered—
> little ones are safe, you know.
>
> —Author unknown

In the final analysis, our little ones won't be safe with values borrowed from us. They must be personally apprehended by the spiritual and moral truths that have gripped our own hearts.

Marital Commitment

The final element of WISDOM is *marital commitment*. In a sense, it's actually the culmination of the other elements we've described. When young people know their worth in God's eyes; when they see integrity modeled in the lives of their parents; when their home offers them security; when they have grasped a sense of their destiny; and when they take ownership of godly values for themselves; then they are well prepared to make a marital commitment that will last a lifetime.

An ounce of parent is worth a pound of psychiatrists.

Today we hear lots of talk about the wounded child still living inside most adults, especially those whose sexuality is broken or whose marriage has failed. But when were all those people wounded in the first place? The injuries were suffered when they were children.

An ounce of *parent* is worth a pound of *psychiatrists*. Doesn't it make sense to do all we can to raise healthy children in the first place so the next generation won't grow up so terribly damaged? By God's grace, we can offer a context of parental WISDOM for our children's growth—providing a fertile soil for the blossoming of their sexuality.

Points to Remember

The final three elements of a healthy context for the key talk are these:

- Destiny—Young people need a purpose in life in order to stay on track.

- Ownership—Children must mature to the place where the values they cherish aren't borrowed from parents or others but rather belong to them personally.
- Marital Commitment—The culmination of all the other elements when a young person has been raised in the wholesome context of WISDOM.

12

Is It Working?

By now you may be thinking, this all sounds like a good idea. But does the key talk work? Amid all the pressures today to become sexually promiscuous, are young people who make such a covenant with God really able to stand strong and keep their promise to be pure?

We must answer those questions with a resounding *yes*. Though of course the key talk (or any other parental strategy, for that matter) can't guarantee that your children will remain virgins till they marry, we can tell you that it has most certainly been effective in our family and in others.

Our four adult children were certainly not sheltered from the world and its temptations. Their commitment to God has been tested and their standards challenged. Yet all four remained virgins till married. More than that, they have grown into strong leaders, influencing other young people to give themselves to godliness.

Up until now we've told you something of what the key talk has meant in our children's walk with God, their life at home, and their stand among their peers. Now it's time to let them tell you those things themselves, from their own perspectives. The following comments come straight from our four children in their own words, from the oldest to the youngest, as well as from some other young people we know. As you read, pay attention not only to what they have to say, but also to the confidence and clarity with which they say it.

Kimberli Durfield (written when twenty-four years old)

It's been over ten years since my mother took me out one special evening and shared the key talk with me. Looking back, I thank God for giving me parents with such wisdom and love. As a young person, I respected my parents more than any other human beings in the world. It was my love and respect for them that opened up my understanding of God's love and care for me.

The years following my key talk were often hard. I was afraid that I would not be able to live up to the commitment I'd made. But I always had in the back of my mind the sacrifice Jesus made for me on the cross, so I knew no sacrifice was too great for me.

Because of my love and desire to please my parents, I refrained from any sexual involvement. But as the years went by, that reason for self-restraint changed. I found that my relationship with Christ grew, and I began to understand more fully the importance of remaining sexually pure before God. It definitely was a decision I grew into.

I thank God that He has continued to be faithful as I face the future, equipped with His grace.

I certainly plan to have a key talk with my own children. I hope to instill in them God's principles and His love. I want my children to know as I did how *important* they are *individually* to God.

Then, when it comes time for them to make their own covenant with God concerning their sexuality, they will be grounded in God's love and assured of our support. I'm sure it will be for them, as it was for me, the best and most important decision they will have made in their lives up to that point.

Does the key talk work for everyone? So much depends upon the example and lifestyle the parents live before the child. It would be very difficult to trust parents in making such a big commitment if you had seen in the past that they hadn't kept their own commitments to God.

I do believe, however, that a child knows when a parent is sincere. So even if a parent hasn't been perfect, if his or her life has been sincere before the child and before God, I believe that the child will respect the parent and will be willing to enter into the covenant.

Anna Durfield (written at twenty-one years old)

I was fourteen when I had my key talk. I believe we had it at just the right time. I guess at the time I really wasn't interested in boys, but I knew all about sex and adolescent body changes.

I was excited to be out with Mom alone. I knew she was looking forward to it herself, so that made my own level of anticipation rise. I knew my older sister had already had a talk years before, and in my mind I had imagined what the key talk would be like. But in reality, the evening turned out somewhat differently from what I had expected.

Mom and I both put on makeup and dressed up nicely that evening. It was such a special evening that to this day I can remember how the restaurant looked and exactly where we sat. I was a little anxious, so my appetite wasn't totally there. We decided to have just some dessert and coffee.

I asked lots of questions about marriage and what it was really like. I had my own ideas about the subject, but I wanted to hear from Mom about it. I asked a multitude of questions about boys and how they work! Mom drew quite a few pictures on napkins explaining sex. We laughed at them—not because they were about sex, but because she's not the greatest artist!

> "I remember that [Mom] said my sexuality was wonderful, God-ordained, and perfect. She also told me I was 100 percent responsible for how I would use this most special and perfect gift."

What do I remember most about what Mom said that night? I remember that she said my sexuality was wonderful, God-ordained, and perfect. She also told me I was 100 percent responsible for how I would use this most special and perfect gift. She said my body was my treasure, and God had given it to me to give to my future husband.

Nothing Mom said that night really shocked me; we've always had a very open relationship in which we were free to talk about such things. The one thing that surprised me, I remember, was how often married couples may have sex—even several times a week. That was so much more often than I would have thought.

I loved the ring! I must have explained its significance to my friends a dozen times. I think all girls love rings, but this one was especially exciting.

As we prayed together, I had a mix of feelings. We've always prayed publicly as a family in restaurants, so I wasn't so concerned about what other people might think as they were looking on. But I did have a sense of excitement about stepping into womanhood, and I had a great sense of strength from Mom's being there with me.

I was very much in agreement with what Mom had to say that evening with regard to sexual standards. I left feeling like I had understood what she wanted to say to me—though since then I've asked a thousand more questions!

In the days following the talk, I remember feeling more adult and more responsible. It made a positive difference in my relationship with my parents: Now that Mom knew all my questions and concerns about sex, I felt that any problems I faced otherwise—at school, church, or wherever—were no big deal for Mom or Dad. They already knew me well and they knew what was on my heart.

The key talk, ring, and covenant have been a constant reminder to me of my commitment to God to remain sexually pure. The ring especially has been a gentle reminder of the Lord through many friendships, and though the friends have come and gone, the ring remains on my finger.

I look forward with excitement to having a key talk with my own children someday. I would also recommend that other families have key talks. I've found that a great amount of healing takes place in the course of the talk—it's a wonderful time of bonding, and it provides a great foundation on which to build a lifetime relationship with your parents.

Timothy Durfield (written at nineteen years old)

Looking back, I can remember the anticipation I felt for that special day when I would have a "handshake" with God by making a covenant with Him. I would make a promise to Him that would last forever. I didn't know exactly what this promise was about, but I knew it was called a "key talk" and that I would sit down with my father and talk about my sexuality. I was really excited, and I remember asking my parents every week when I could have my key talk.

Finally the night came. My dad took me to a classy restaurant, and when we were seated, he told me I could order whatever I wanted. At that point I was really nervous: I had thought we would sit down and start talking about this key talk right away. Instead, my father waited to begin until we had ordered and almost finished our meal. This was a perfect time, because by then I was more relaxed, and we had already been talking about everyday things for the past hour.

The focus of the conversation that night was that my body was the temple of God. My father stressed that the Holy Spirit lives in me. So whatever I participate in—whether sexual immorality, alcohol abuse, or foul language—I bring that activity into God's dwelling place, which is me.

Nothing Dad said that night really came as a shock or even a surprise to me. He was very straightforward. After we talked, I knew clearly the reasons why God wanted me to keep myself sexually pure until I was married. I also knew that if I made a covenant with God, I'd better keep it. And if I kept it, God would not only help me but also bless me because of my faithfulness.

The excitement grew when Dad asked me to pray. I, Timothy Durfield, was going to make a deal with God! I wanted to be good, not only for God, but also for my dad and mom, who cared enough to tell me what God wanted from me.

When the covenant was made, I thought, "Now it's final." I could see a big smile on God's face because He and I had a special bond that would last forever. My dad then presented me with a ring—God's ring.

That ring meant a lot to me because I knew it represented a strong stand. When two people are married, not only a verbal commitment is given, but also a ring, a symbol of their commitment. So now, I thought, from here on out, whatever I set my hands to, that promise sitting on my finger—that key ring—will be looking me straight in the eye. And the promise would be not only to keep me from doing wrong, but also to bless my hands in whatever I would do.

I plan to have a key talk with my children, and I would recommend that other families do the same with each of their kids. When a family makes a decision together to honor God, a spiritual bond is woven throughout the family, and God ties a knot, causing all things to work together for good.

Although the key talk is a valuable tool, dads should also remember that God instructs fathers not to provoke their children to wrath but to bring them up in the discipline and instruction of the Lord (Eph. 6:4). I'm nineteen years old now and away at college, thousands of miles from home. But even now I need my father's insight and instruction to keep me on that narrow path that will lead me to victory in Jesus Christ.

Jonathan Durfield (written at seventeen years old)

I had my key talk when I was fifteen years old. Looking back now, I think that was the right time for me. I was just entering the stage of being interested in the opposite sex.

My thoughts in the days before the key talk were full of excitement. My brother and sisters had something special, and I wanted what they had. I understood basically what the talk was about, but I was still excited because I knew it would bring my father and me closer together, and that made me happy.

I felt very important because Dad had taken time out of his busy schedule to talk with me. His willingness to devote this special time and energy to the key talk impressed me with the seriousness and importance of the evening.

I still remember clearly how the waitress seated us, not in a private corner somewhere as we'd requested, but in a table right in the middle of the restaurant. I knew that everyone could see what we were doing there.

Nothing Dad said that night shocked me. I'd had lots of chances before to learn basic facts about sex from many sources: open conversations with Mom, open talks with my older brother and sisters, high school health class, and our church youth group. My big questions that night had to do with sex and dating. Where was the line between right and wrong? How far should I go with a girl on a date? I wanted details. Dad's responses to my questions seemed agreeable and reasonable.

The ring impressed me as a special gift from Dad. I was overjoyed to receive it and to wear it proudly.

As Dad and I prayed in the restaurant with other people looking on, I thought, If I'm going to make a covenant this strong, I might as well go all out and take a public stand with it. No matter what anyone says, I told myself, God is more important to me than their opinions.

In the years since the key talk, I have found that it has led to a closer relationship with God and a stronger will to resist temptation. It has also helped me have a greater understanding of who God is and how much He really cares about me.

I believe the key talk also brought me closer to my father. It gave me a new understanding of him and opened a new door of communication between us. It helped us build a real friendship.

I certainly plan to have key talks with my own kids some-day—in helping young people remain sexually pure, I think it's the only way to go. In fact, I believe all parents would do well to have key talks with their children. Raising a child is a hard task—and parents need all the help they can get!

Other young people we know:

Billy (twenty years old)

Ten years ago, the Durfields encouraged my parents to have key talks with the children in our family. As it turned out, you might say I had my key talk in several "stages" over a period of years.

First, when I was in the sixth grade, Dad took me aside to have a "birds and bees talk." I had no idea what that meant. Dad said, "Don't you want to know about how babies are made?"

"No!" I said emphatically.

"Well," said Dad, "I'm going to tell you anyway."

It seems funny now. But I still remember that Dad made it clear how important this subject was, and his seriousness made a big impact on me.

When I was in the tenth grade, Dad took me out to a restaurant for a special night out, and I was thrilled to have him all to myself for an evening. Once again, my father began talking about sex, and in particular about some of his own experiences as a young man. At first, I didn't understand what was going on. But I do remember well the primary point my father made that evening: "Son, keep yourself pure and stay a virgin." He was quite clear about what was right and what was wrong.

I felt so honored that night to be talking "man to man" with my father. It made me feel special and made Dad and me closer friends.

Finally, in my freshman year of college, my parents called me into the living room to talk. I thought I might be in trouble. Instead, they presented me with a beautiful gold covenant ring.

My mother began to talk about sexual purity, so I said, "Mom, I've already had this talk."

"When?" Dad asked.

"In the tenth grade at the restaurant." The little talk we'd had on that special night out had made a greater impression on me than Dad had realized.

I'm twenty now and in my second year of college, and I'm still a virgin. When people first notice my ring, they always comment on how beautiful it is. So I take the opportunity to tell them what it represents. My friends respect me for the stand I take.

I don't seek a wide circle of friends; I enjoy having a few close Christian friends who share my commitment. I do talk with non-Christians about where I stand, especially when locker room discussions about sex come up. But I don't attack them for their lack of standards.

I believe that young people should have a key talk at an early age to plant a good seed within them. If the child doesn't understand everything, it can be repeated again a few years later, as my parents did with me. Our society will certainly be pressuring the young person to act irresponsibly before he or she understands what it's all about, so we have to provide the counterpressure.

This is especially the case considering the rampant spread of STDs. Young people need to know early on that having sex outside marriage is like playing Russian roulette.

I believe there's a unique power to the key talk covenant. When you make a promise to Jesus, your parents, and your spouse-to-be, then much more is on the line if you break it. I've felt a special grace to trust God to help me remain pure till He brings my wife along at the right time.

> "I believe there's a unique power to the key talk covenant. . . . I've felt a special grace to trust God to help me remain pure till He brings my wife along at the right time."

"Wendy" (nineteen years old)

I was raised in a Christian home where godly morals were clearly taught and emphasized. As I was growing up, my parents always answered openly and honestly any question I had about sex. But during those early years, we never had an in-depth discussion of sexual issues and the sexual problems the current generation faces.

I had lots of close male friends but no single "boyfriend." I felt I was not as pretty as most other girls and that maybe I wasn't "good enough" to have a boyfriend. Even so, all in all I was a happy, well-adjusted high schooler, and I have good memories of that time.

When I was fifteen and in the tenth grade, my girl friends began telling me about their sexual encounters. At that time I had made a commitment to God to stay sexually pure. I remembered all that my parents had told me about holiness, and I told God, "My virginity is too important to throw away." I didn't realize till later, when I met the Durfields, the magnitude of the covenant I'd made, or how important it would become to me.

Finally I met a young man in whom I sensed a security, a pureness, and a love for the Lord. Up until that time, I'd really been afraid of boys. But this one just wanted to be my friend, and in time he became my boyfriend.

This special friend had made the key talk covenant with God to remain pure. So we can tell you that the power to resist sexual temptation is more than doubled when the person you're dating is as committed as you are to purity. For us, there's just no question about going too far. If one of us gets "overheated," the other cools the situation down. Both of us know the rules, and we've stayed within those rules.

I believe it's very important to date only Christians. It's too rough to date non-Christians, because in the secular world there aren't any boundaries in this area. In the heat of passion, it would be hard to stop if both people involved didn't have the same rules. It's especially important that the guy be a Christian, because a guy can push his desires on a girl.

When the day comes that I have my own children, I definitely plan to have the key talk with them. And I want to have it early enough so they'll know they can come to me to discuss questions about sexuality freely, whenever those questions should arise.

Has the key talk made a critical difference in the lives of these young people? We think their comments speak for themselves. We're truly humbled by what God has done to keep them faithful to Him. And we look forward with them to the time when we'll see *their* children walking tall and confident, wearing their own special key rings with pride.

Points to Remember

The young people who recalled their key talk experience here made several important points:

- The key talk made them feel special and brought them closer to their parents and to God.
- The key talk was useful both for providing information about sex and for clarifying moral issues.
- The ring had meaning both as a reminder of the covenant and as a catalyst for conversations with peers about the key talk.
- All the young people who participated in the key talk were so convinced of its effectiveness that they plan to have it with their own children.

13

Special Hurdles

Sometimes our best efforts to protect our children from sexual sin fail. We've known Christian couples who were model parents in all the ways we've described in this book— yet their hearts were broken one day to discover that their teenage daughter was pregnant or that their son had contracted HIV.

We encourage parents not to wait too long to have the key talk with their child. Children in our society are being introduced to sex by their peers and by the mass media much earlier than in previous generations. Yet even when the key talk is held with a young teenager, a parent may be hurt and dismayed to find that the child has already fallen into sexual sin.

This chapter is especially for families who have some tough hurdles to overcome—either because a child is reluctant to make the key talk covenant, or because a child is already dealing with the consequences of sexual immorality. Here are some questions that reflect what we believe to be the more difficult of those situations, and our suggestions for responding to each.

1. What should I do if my child resists the idea of a key talk?

First, you need to educate your child to the terrible risks of sex outside of marriage. Some people might write this approach off as a "fear tactic," and we must agree that it would be better for a child to be motivated out of a desire to be holy. Nevertheless, the destructive consequences of promiscuity are real, and sometimes we have to start with obeying God out of fear before we can learn to obey Him out of love.

Begin by talking with your child about the health risks of sex before marriage, discussing the deadly effects of AIDS and the debilitating effects of other STDs. To educate your child more thoroughly, try reading a book, watching a video, or attending a lecture together on the subject. You might even want to talk with hospital personnel or victims of STDs who are anxious to warn others of the danger.

Seek to be a spiritual role model in your home, so that your child can see firsthand what a genuine believer is.

Second, you need to search the Scriptures together with your child to examine the biblical view of sexual misconduct and its spiritual and psychological consequences. A good place to begin is 1 Corinthians 6:13–20 and Romans 1. Further relevant biblical texts can be found in the back of this book.

Stress the biblical truths that God forbids sexual immorality because it injures our psychological and spiritual natures. Sexual union is not merely physical. It also causes a bonding with the other person at a deep level of our being that is healthy if that person is our lifelong marriage partner, but if it takes place outside of marriage it becomes a destructive bondage.

The third part of a long-term strategy in this situation is to encourage your child toward a vital relationship with the Lord. Share the love of Christ with your child, especially by your own example. Seek to be a spiritual role model in your home, so that your child can see firsthand what a genuine believer is. Church attendance and involvement in a vibrantly alive Christian youth ministry are also critical in this regard.

2. What should I do in the key talk if my child rejects the Bible as an authoritative guide for life?

First, remember that the need for fervent intercession in this situation cannot be overemphasized.

Second, keep in mind that even if your child rejects biblical authority, you can use factual information from outside the Bible that will still make an impact on your child's understanding of how serious a matter sexual involvement is. Provide information about AIDS and other STDs. Cite the statistics from the first chapter in this book that show how many children who are born outside of marriage end up in conditions of poverty. Talk about the physical and emotional dangers of abortion. You may even find people who have made mistakes in this area who are willing to talk about the devastating consequences of their choices.

Use marriage as an illustration of how even the secular world, which doesn't recognize biblical authority, nevertheless has adopted biblical principles for successful family life. You can talk about marriage in non-biblical terms if you must by discussing it as a commitment—a covenant between two people who love each other and desire to spend the rest of their lives together and to provide a secure environment for children to be reared.

The key talk covenant is in a sense an extension of the marriage vow, made prior to actually meeting the person to be married. If your child believes he or she will someday make a commitment to be faithful to one person in marriage, why not enter into the spirit of that marriage covenant even now for the sake of the person to be married one day?

You can also find other young people who have made the commitment to remain sexually pure and arrange for them to meet with your child. Perhaps a group of your child's peers might make a greater impact.

3. What should I do if my child tells me in the key talk that he or she is no longer a virgin?

Your child needs to know that some of the greatest figures in the Bible, like King David, Mary Magdalene, the apostle Peter, and the apostle Paul, also failed God. But they were willing to seek His forgiveness and turn from their sin back to Him.

God's forgiveness is as perfect and complete as He is. God says in the Bible to those who receive His forgiveness, "I will forgive their iniquity, and I will remember their sin no more" (Jer. 31:34). King David was so confident the Lord was willing to forgive every sin he'd ever committed that he even asked God to forgive the sins of his youth (Ps. 25:7).

With God, there is no such thing as partial forgiveness. Either He refuses to forgive, or He forgives completely. The Bible tells us that "if we confess our sins, He is faithful and just to forgive us our sins, and to cleanse us from *all* unrighteousness" (1 John 1:9, emphasis added).

The Scriptures record that Ahab, Jezebel's husband, was one of the most wicked kings ever to rule over Israel: "There was never a man like Ahab, who sold himself to do evil in the eyes of the Lord, urged on by Jezebel, his wife. He behaved in the vilest manner by going after idols" (1 Kings 21:25 NIV).

Nevertheless, as evil as he was, when Ahab turned away from his wickedness, God spared him from judgment. No matter how badly we have sinned, God will forgive us if we're willing to repent—to turn away from our sin.

The apostle Paul told us: "If anyone is in Christ, he is a new creation; the old has gone, the new has come" (2 Cor. 5:17 NIV). So as a forgiven child of God who is in Christ, your child can consider him or herself what we call a "secondary virgin." That is, your child's key talk commitment to purity begins at the time of forgiveness, when he or she is washed clean by God and made new, and it continues until your child enters the covenant of marriage.

4. What should I do if my child tells me during the key talk that he or she is homosexual?

This kind of revelation can be unsettling to a parent. But keep in mind that if your child should share such an intimate secret with you, this confession indicates a level of trust that will allow you to lovingly pursue a solution to the dilemma.

In this situation, your child needs to know above all that you love him or her unconditionally. God's love and your love for your child aren't nullified simply because he or she feels homosexual tendencies or has engaged in homosexual behavior. Nor does a homosexual orientation mean your child does not need to make a firm commitment to abstain from sex outside of marriage.

You'll want to find out exactly what your child means when he or she claims to be homosexual. Has your child had occasional feelings of attraction to the same sex along with more constant heterosexual attraction, or has it been a lifelong, exclusive homosexual orientation? Has your child actually engaged in homosexual behavior? If so, what kind of behavior and how often? Was your child ever seduced into a homosexual act by an older person?

These questions are important because they will help you determine the extent of the problem. Homosexuality varies in intensity and expression. Some young people may unnecessarily fear that they're homosexual simply because they've been occasionally attracted to an adult of the same sex (this issue was discussed in an earlier chapter). Others may have had only a single homosexual experience, such as group masturbation among several boys, that was more an occasion of experimentation than attraction (though the act was of course still sinful). Still others may have experienced fleeting same-sex attractions yet most of the time feel heterosexually oriented.

If the extent of homosexual feelings or behavior has been limited and heterosexual attraction is otherwise strong, then you can encourage your child that his or her primary orientation is heterosexual. Explain that a few isolated homosexual feelings or behaviors don't make a person homosexual. You should talk about any negative feelings your child may have toward the opposite sex that may make him or her feel awkward or threatened in boy-girl relationships. This kind of discussion may help your child overcome such feelings.

As we discussed in an earlier chapter, homosexual acts are a sin, and if your child has engaged in such activity, he or she needs to repent and receive forgiveness. But if your child has resisted the temptation to engage in overt sexual behaviors, then he or she should be encouraged that homosexual feelings or even a homosexual orientation are not in themselves sinful.

If your child is having strong and persistent same-sex feelings, he or she needs emotional healing. We would urge you to root your child firmly in the Lord through the help and counsel of a pastor, Christian counselor, or even an organization designed to minister to those who want to overcome a homosexual lifestyle (see the listings in the back of this book). You should also seek to remove your child from any friends or environment that would influence him or her toward a homosexual lifestyle.

In the meantime, you and your child should read together and discuss some of the Christian literature currently available that deals with this subject (again, see the list of resources at the back of this book). As you study, you'll probably be most concerned about two issues: the causes of homosexuality and the possibility of sexual reorientation.

The causes of homosexuality have been debated in scientific and theological circles. Some scientific evidence implicates environmental factors such as unhealthy parent-child relationships or childhood trauma (including sexual abuse). Other findings point more toward the possibility of prenatal, chemical, or genetic influences that might predispose some people to homosexuality.

With regard to the possibility of change, some mental health professionals insist that in many cases, the homosexual orientation can be partially or totally overcome when the patient is highly motivated. A number of Christians who once lived a homosexual lifestyle testify that their faith has given them that kind of strong motivation. Some say that their orientation has become completely heterosexual; many have married happily and become parents. Others cannot make that claim, but they say that God has nevertheless given them victory over sinful homosexual behavior.

In any case, we can say that whatever the cause of a person's homosexual orientation, that person is not doomed to a life of sexual failure. By God's grace, even those with the strongest homosexual inclinations can learn to live a life that is pleasing to God.

5. What should I do if my child tells me during the key talk that he or she has an STD?

The problems caused by STDs can affect so many people that an infected person really has no choice but to seek professional care and counsel. This is for the safety of the person infected as well as the safety of others. The impact of an STD, like that of a pregnancy, goes far beyond the sexually involved couple. Friends, family, and future sexual partners are deeply affected, as are the children born ill or deformed by such a disease.

Beyond the physical ramifications of STDs are the spiritual ones, which require a response similar to what we've described in the answers to the previous two questions. Forgiveness from God is certain if your child experiences true godly sorrow, resulting in complete repentance. The

Scriptures are quite clear about God's acceptance of those who have failed but come to Him in brokenness.

The issues involving your child's other relationships, however, are a different matter. If your child has waited until the key talk to tell you about having an STD, you must ask yourself why he or she waited until now. Was it because of a fear of rejection? Did your child think there was no avenue of communication open?

Whatever the case, the very fact that your child mustered up enough courage to share this information with Mom or Dad at the key talk indicates that he or she views this occasion as an unprecedented opportunity to open up. So you should take advantage of the occasion to talk together freely and honestly and to assist your child in this matter of great need.

You should assure your child that you'll do everything in your power to help him or her through this terribly painful and embarrassing experience. Also let your child know you'll protect his or her privacy while seeking various avenues of help.

The commitment to sexual purity by a child who has an STD should be no different from the covenant made by anyone else in the key talk. The parent should feel free to lead the child in prayer for forgiveness and then in a prayer of commitment, sealing the covenant with the ring.

If your child's disease is medically incurable—such as genital herpes or even AIDS—then you and your child must address together some further issues: Can you pray that God would heal the disease, or must it be borne as some sort of punishment? In the case of a disease like genital herpes, how does your child go about discussing it with a potential mate, and at what stage in the relationship? In the case of AIDS, how do you prepare for the prospect of death?

The answers to the last questions are highly individual, so we can only raise the issues and allow those who must wrestle with them to seek God for wisdom. But we should note in regard to the first question that we believe it's always appropriate to pray for healing, whatever the cause of an illness. Though AIDS or any other STD might, in fact, have come as the natural *consequence* of sexual sin, we don't believe that a Christian who has genuinely repented and asked God for forgiveness must be resigned to accepting the condition as a divine punishment.

6. What should I do if my daughter tells me during the talk that she has had an abortion?

Again, the same principles of repentance and forgiveness apply in this case as in other cases of sexual failure. However, you have in addition a few special issues to deal with: Why was your child unwilling to tell you about the abortion before now? Does your daughter fully understand the seriousness of having taken an unborn child's life?

The emotional aftermath of an abortion can be devastating as a woman (or girl) begins to consider the horror of what has taken place. One study of women who'd had abortions showed:

- Eighty-one percent reported preoccupation with the aborted child.
- Seventy-three percent reported flashbacks of the abortion experience.
- Sixty-nine percent reported feelings of "craziness" after the abortion.

- Fifty-four percent recalled nightmares related to abortion.
- Thirty-five percent reported "visitations" from the aborted child.
- Twenty-three percent reported hallucinations related to the abortion.

If your child, with your help, seems unable to work through the guilt and grief resulting from an abortion and find a place of forgiveness (including self-forgiveness) and peace of mind, seek professional Christian counseling. You may also get assistance from ministries that care for sufferers of post-abortion trauma.

7. **What if I have sexual sin in my own past that makes me feel guilty and hypocritical in having a key talk? It also makes me doubt whether the ideal of purity can realistically be maintained. How do I deal with my own feelings?**

Just as your child must receive God's forgiveness for any previous sexual misconduct, so must you. The Bible tells us: "Therefore, there is now no condemnation for those who are in Christ Jesus" (Rom. 8:1 NIV). Condemnation is never of God when you have repented of past sins. God *convicts* us of sin, but it's Satan who *condemns* us for what we've done wrong.

The apostle Paul once told the secret of his ability to minister despite his past as a rebellious enemy of God: "Forgetting what is behind and straining toward what is ahead, I press on toward the goal to win the prize for which God has called me heavenward in Christ Jesus" (Phil. 3:13–14 NIV). Parents who have failed must also forget the past and press toward the goals God has placed before them—including the prize of seeing their children grow up to be whole people and godly parents who are happily married.

It's never helpful to dwell on past failures. Instead, we must focus on God-given goals we can pursue with excitement.

If you have totally repented of your past, it's not at all hypocritical to challenge your child to a biblical standard of holiness. In fact, those who are most keenly aware of their own failures and of God's great mercy are in a good position to share with their children the great love of God that deserves our total commitment. As Jesus once said, the one who has been forgiven much loves much (see Luke 7:36–50).

Perhaps when you were young, you had no one to encourage you to commit yourself to sexual purity. If not, take this as an opportunity to give your child what you didn't have so he or she can avoid the mistakes you made.

Absolute sexual abstinence outside of marriage is certainly a realistic standard, and the possibility of your child achieving that standard has nothing to do with your own past. If anything, your child has a much better opportunity to remain pure because he or she has your encouragement and support through the key talk covenant.

Remember that God would not require of us what we're unable to accomplish. We have this promise: "His divine power has given us everything we need for life and godliness through our knowledge of him who called us by his own glory and goodness" (2 Peter 1:3 NIV). Many people have held firmly to biblical sexual standards for a lifetime, and they can testify to God's faithfulness in this regard.

8. If I have sexual sin in my own past, should I tell my child about it?

We believe that it's unwise to let your child know that you've failed sexually in the past if that's the case. We don't think it's necessary to rehearse all the details of your failures; that certainly won't serve the purposes of the key talk, and it might even be harmful. The point to emphasize is that all of us—parents and children alike—are totally dependent upon God; He has forgiven all our trespasses, and He stands ready to forgive us again if we ever fall.

9. What if my child breaks the covenant after the key talk?

The conditions that govern our relationship to Christ in our covenant of salvation also govern our relationship to Him in other covenant agreements such as marriage. The Bible encourages us to "approach the throne of grace with confidence, so that we may receive mercy and find grace to help us in our time of need" (Heb. 4:16 NIV).

Mercy is for the guilty and grace is for the helpless. Even in a secular setting, the guilty may throw themselves on the mercy of the court. How much more, then, should we be able to throw ourselves on God's mercy as we approach His throne?

We must encourage our children never to forget that God has promised to stand by them always and to guide them through every circumstance they may face. Jesus is the Friend who "sticks closer than a brother" (Prov. 18:24). He will always be there to lift them when they fall, just as He was there to lift the apostle Peter when Peter's doubt caused him to begin sinking beneath the waves of the stormy sea (Matt. 14:28–31).

Whatever our child's situation—even if it's an out-of-wedlock pregnancy, an STD infection, a homosexual orientation, or the aftermath of abortion—we must remember that the Lord came to earth for the very purpose of forgiving and delivering us. How could He possibly forsake us when we need forgiveness and deliverance the most?

Points to Remember

- If your child resists the key talk:

  1. Educate him or her to the dangers of sex outside of marriage.
  2. Search the Scriptures together to examine God's view of sexual misconduct.
  3. Encourage your child toward a vital relationship with the Lord.

- If your child confesses to sexual sin during the key talk, help him or her confess it to God and receive forgiveness. If necessary, seek professional help in dealing with STDs, homosexuality, and the aftermath of abortion.

- If you have sexual sin in your own past, don't let it hinder you from having a key talk with your child. Receive God's forgiveness and make it your intent to give your child the support you may never have had.

14

Beyond the Teen Years

Sexual purity is, of course, not just for teens. Nor is the key talk idea just for parents. Any single person who desires to walk in holiness can benefit from making a covenant with God to remain sexually pure. And the person who makes such a covenant can be supported in it by any Christian relative, friend, pastor, or mentor who is willing to stand alongside as an "advocate" in the battle against temptation.

For that reason, our four children aren't the only ones we've supported in making a key talk covenant. A number of others—friends of our children, older singles, divorced people, single parents—have come to us as well, asking if we would stand with them in making a promise to God that they would remain sexually pure. For these folks we've come to serve as "surrogate parents."

No doubt many young men, for example, don't have a dad around to give them a key talk. But they may have an uncle, a grandfather, a youth pastor, or an adult friend who has earned their trust and could fill that role instead. Or consider how many unwed mothers wanting to get back on track in their spiritual life might welcome the support of an older

> **"'Surrogate parents' can provide the single person with the essentials of the key talk idea: loving support, a place to discuss sexual issues openly, a source of wisdom and counsel, and a point of accountability."**

Christian woman who can offer wisdom and encouragement.

Whatever the particulars of the situation, we believe the key talk idea can be adapted to fit. Some people might need very little information about sexuality, yet they hunger to have someone hold them accountable in a specific commitment to God. Others might need special help in studying the Scriptures to understand more fully the spiritual dimension of their sexuality so they can overcome the notion that God is just an arbitrary rule maker. Still others might need someone to help them unravel the sexual tragedies of the past so they can receive emotional healing.

In every case, we believe that "surrogate parents" can provide the single person with the essentials of the key talk idea: loving support, a place to discuss sexual issues openly, a source of biblical wisdom and counsel, and a point of accountability.

To illustrate the variety of situations that would benefit from adapting the key talk, we want to tell the stories of a few people beyond the teen years who are grateful they made the covenant. The names and some of the details have been changed in order to protect the privacy of those involved.

Steve

Steve is a handsome single in his twenties. He was raised in a Christian home, and his parents provided him with clear moral teaching about sexual issues. Through junior and senior high school he maintained the standards he'd been taught.

Near the end of high school, however, Steve was in a bad accident while drinking. His injuries laid him up all summer long, and he grew bitter toward God for allowing the accident to happen.

During his first years in college, Steve got a job, and his co-workers there influenced him toward continued drinking. They also talked frequently about sex and would question his claim to be a virgin. "You've never had sex?" they asked. "You're so good-looking, we thought for sure you loved the ladies." In addition, he discovered that an old friend he'd grown up with in church was himself quite sexually active, which only added to the doubts he'd begun to have about his standards.

Meanwhile, Steve met a woman who was a few years his senior and in college also. She made a project of seducing him, and within eight weeks he lost his virginity at the age of eighteen. He never saw her again after that night.

Soon this young man's mind was consumed with sexual thoughts. He found that taking part in the constant talk of his friends about sex grew addictive like a drug. He walked farther and farther away from God until he was deaf to His voice.

Steve continued drinking and partying, and he took up smoking. While under the influence of alcohol and cocaine, he had four more sexual encounters in the following two years. The drugs contributed heavily to the weakening of his moral standards.

Nevertheless, when Steve was twenty he recommitted his life to the Lord. Subsequently, through the key talk he made a covenant with God to remain sexually pure. He later began dating a Christian girl who is a virgin and is also committed to sexual purity.

During the time Steve and this young woman dated, they often encountered situations when it was tough to resist sexual temptation. But looking back, Steve can identify several reasons they were able to remain pure:

- After making the covenant, he had a new respect for God and a keen sense of the guilt he would feel if he broke God's law.

- He also had a new respect for his girlfriend's virginity, recognizing that he had no right to take it.

- Whenever the sexual pressure was on, God reminded him of the covenant he'd made.

- The couple made it a habit to pray together, especially toward the end of the evening when they were alone together.

- They also learned to avoid the situations that left them most vulnerable to temptation: being alone together in an apartment or parked in a car; late-night dates; times when they were fatigued and their resistance to temptation was low.

Today, Steve has continued to keep his covenant with God. When the day comes that he has his own children, he wants to have a key talk with them as well.

Why? Steve recognizes that even though his parents were clear about moral standards when he was young, they were embarrassed to talk about sex with him. Consequently, most of his sex education came from public school teachers, locker-room talk, and friends. He hopes to provide his own children with an advantage he lacked: a "safe" place at home to talk about sex and to draw support and encouragement in the commitment to remain pure.

Tammy

Tammy was only fifteen years old when she had sex for the first time. She was with two young men and an eighteen-year-old cousin who convinced her that sex outside marriage was okay and that she didn't need to worry about getting pregnant. She remembers the evening as a terrible and empty experience.

When Tammy was sixteen, she had sex several times with one particular boy, and she eventually became pregnant by him. During the pregnancy she was rejected by her closest friends and experienced some deep hurts. But she drew closer to her parents, who became her best friends and supporters.

About six months into the pregnancy, Tammy made a key talk covenant with God to abstain from sex again until marriage. She received a beautiful silver ring as a reminder of her commitment. She faithfully kept her promise to the Lord, and now, as a young adult, she has a wonderful Christian husband and a beautiful child.

Tammy believes that if her mom had had the key talk with her when she was thirteen or fourteen, that cousin would never have been able to persuade her to have sex. She feels that the ring, which held special meaning for her, would have been a forceful reminder of her commitment. Nevertheless, she appreciates having been encouraged to make the covenant when she did to keep her safe until the right man came along. Someday she hopes to have a key talk with her child and to serve as a surrogate parent to other young girls who need support.

Melissa

Melissa is a beautiful girl we met on one of our ministry trips in another country. As a young child and a teenager, Melissa was intensely devoted to God. She was a strong believer in obeying His Word and was totally unblemished in her sexual life.

Nevertheless, she remembers having negative thoughts about sex planted in her mind from an early age. She thought of her body as "dirty." To make matters worse, her parents divorced when she was a child, and her mother wasn't able to support her in developing emotional stability or a healthy thought life.

In Melissa's last year of high school she met a boy who became very special to her. He seemed like such a "sweet" young man. But he had been physically and emotionally battered by his parents, and in time he physically abused Melissa. He repeatedly raped her anally and forced her to engage in oral sex with him. He frightened her into submission by threatening to tell her parents. Yet he also pleaded with her to remain with him because he "loved" her.

After high school, Melissa met a young man who was kind and seemed to love her. At the age of eighteen she chose to have vaginal intercourse with him for the first time. Then, about a year and a half into the relationship, she got pregnant.

The couple agreed that they would not get married but would have an abortion. He agreed to pay for the procedure, which took place "no questions asked" when she was three months into the pregnancy. About six months later, the relationship ended, but the painful memory of the abortion continued.

In time, Melissa realized that her life was on a destructive course, and she concluded that she should make a covenant with God to be sexually pure. She sealed the covenant with a key ring on her finger, which she bought in a style heavy enough to make sure she would be continually aware of its presence.

Today, Melissa recognizes that she has "a strong desire to be tenderly loved." But she has kept her promise to God. She says she has learned to rely on God's love first, and she keeps in mind the consequences of sin.

Melissa was helped so much by the key ring covenant that she recommends it strongly to parents. She believes it can help them provide a protective covering of love and watchful care for their children.

Inside Melissa's ring these words are engraved: "My love for God, my love for you." When she had those words etched there, she had no one in sight for a possible mate. Yet she was confident that God would provide the right person at the right time.

Today she and a beautiful young man are making plans for their eventual union as husband and wife. Through prayer, patience, and her covenant promise, the tragedy of Melissa's early life has been transformed into a testimony to God's faithfulness.

Tyra

Tyra is a beautiful black woman in her forties, the divorced mother of a teenager. Seven years after her divorce, she made a key ring covenant with God. She has kept that commitment to sexual purity, and it has allowed her to walk with integrity before her daughter—with whom she has also had a key talk.

Tyra offers some insights especially for divorced women who must operate in the business world. She notes that because she is single, she has to protect herself from advances by the men she works with. In our society, many men think they can say just about anything to a divorced woman and get away with it. A woman must be aware of her emotional state to avoid falling for manipulative compliments from the opposite sex and must be quick to let men know when she thinks their comments are inappropriate.

Recently, for example, a man in Tyra's office was dressed exceptionally well, and she commented, "You really look nice today. Are you going somewhere special?" The man replied that he was going to meet his girlfriend for a date.

Then he added with a smirk: "You know what they say. You take them for dinner and they'll give you dessert."

Tyra responded immediately. "That's *very* offensive to me," she said. "If your girlfriend knew what you just said, I'm sure she wouldn't go out with you." The man blushed with shame and apologized.

Tyra is adamant that single women who have promised to remain sexually pure must steer clear of that kind of talk. "Why," she asks, "do so many women feel helpless when others push them into inappropriate conversation? We've got to realize that we don't owe such people anything—certainly not the courtesy of listening."

On another occasion, a man eighteen years her junior walked past Tyra's office and told her how nice she looked. She said a simple "Thanks" and smiled. But he took that as an opportunity to go a step further.

"Who's your man?" he asked.

Tyra looked at him sternly and said: "I'm old enough to be your mother. Would you like someone to ask your mother that question?" The man quickly apologized.

In that situation, Tyra recalls, she couldn't afford to let him influence her with a compliment. The man thought she was open game because she was divorced and probably had strong sexual needs. So he used her kindness toward him to try to take advantage of her. But as on so many other occasions, her covenant with God helped keep her strong.

How would Tyra sum up her advice to other single and divorced women? She recommends:

- Make that covenant with God to remain sexually pure until God sees fit to bring along the right person for you. Pray together with a spiritual leader you trust, covering all the basics of the key talk. Wear the ring to symbolize your covenant.

- Watch what you read. Avoid sensual romance novels, women's magazines with sexually stimulating material, and articles on sex for married women.

- Watch television, movies, and videos with discretion. Even the talk on game shows is filled with sexual innuendo and coarse jokes. Watching romantic movies can make you dissatisfied with your own current lot in life. Guard your mind and thoughts!

- Avoid conversations heading in the wrong direction. Walk away from unwholesome talk, even if it seems impolite to do so.

- Be extremely selective in your friendships—even with Christians you can have problems in this area.

- Dress conservatively. If you don't, you leave yourself open to comments from men and even other women who think you're sexually loose. Married women in particular may feel threatened if you dress provocatively around their husbands, and this could cut you off from the friendship of married couples—a support singles often need.

These few stories of people who have made the key ring covenant provide convincing evidence that the commitment can yield benefits even when it's initiated beyond the teen years. If you're an older single who wishes your parents had had a key talk with you when you were young, remember: It's never too late to make a covenant with God. Go to a spiritual leader you trust, explain the idea of the key ring covenant, and ask that person to pray with you and stand with you in your commitment. Wear a ring to symbolize your promise to God, and let it remind you daily that God's perfect will is always worth waiting for.

On the other hand, perhaps you know of a situation in which you could become a "surrogate parent" for someone else in need of an advocate. Ask God to show you if you're the person to meet that need. You may find the role a challenging one—but you'll never find it short of precious rewards when you gain the privilege of helping a child of God walk in purity and power.

Points to Remember

- The key talk can be adapted to fit the needs of people beyond the teen years who want support in making a covenant to be sexually pure before God.
- Older singles, divorced people, unmarried mothers, and others who desire the benefits of a key talk covenant should seek out a trusted spiritual leader to stand with them in their commitment.
- Mature Christians should be alert to situations in which they could serve as "surrogate parents" to someone who needs the key talk.

15

The Power of Purity

A Jewish comedian once told the story of the old man—himself Jewish—who visited the delicatessen to buy something for his dinner. Peering through the meat case, he carefully reviewed his options, then made up his mind.

"A quarter-pound of the corned beef," he said, pointing to an item in the corner.

Gently, the woman behind the counter said, "I'm sorry, sir, but that's ham."

The customer bristled. "And who," he said, "asked *you*?"

All of us at times tend to be like the old man in the story. We want people to tell us only what we want to hear. The truth is often much too disturbing.

Just now we feel a bit like the woman behind the counter in that deli. As we talk to parents about the world their children are facing, we don't enjoy telling them of the dangers. But we believe we must—so they can take action to protect the ones they love.

Some years ago, a newspaper carried a dismal report about a survey conducted in fifty cities around the nation. More than two thousand people were asked to reveal their thoughts about a number of moral issues, with anonymity guaranteed. The results were unsettling, if not surprising.

- Only 13 percent of those surveyed still believe in all the Ten Commandments.
- Nine out of ten lie regularly.
- Nearly a third of those married have had an affair.
- A fifth of the young people surveyed lost their virginity by the age of thirteen.
- For ten million dollars, 25 percent would abandon their families, 23 percent would become a prostitute for a week, and 7 percent would murder a stranger.
- Among the "ten sleaziest ways to make a living," TV evangelists, congressmen, and local politicians ranked alongside prostitutes, drug dealers, and organized crime bosses.

One recent study of television-show content concluded that the typical young person sees and hears some fifteen thousand references to sex on TV every year.

On the same page of the paper, an FBI report claimed that violent crime—murder, rape, robbery, and aggravated assault—had jumped 10 percent.

The moral fabric of our nation is fast unraveling. And we must raise our children to stand strong in the face of the tangle of immorality.

We know that's not an easy task by any means. The pressures on our children to compromise are relent-

218

less. The Joint Statement on the Impact of Entertainment Violence on Children released by the Congressional Public Health Summit, July 26, 2002, indicated: "At this time, well over 1,000 studies—including reports from the Surgeon General's office, the National Institute of Mental Health, and numerous studies conducted by leading figures within our medical and public health organizations—our own members—point overwhelmingly to a causal connection between media violence and aggressive behavior in some children. The conclusion of the public health community, based on over 30 years of research, is that viewing entertainment violence can lead to increases in aggressive attitudes, values and behavior, particularly in children."

Are We Hoping for Too Much?

In light of such disturbing realities, some parents might wonder whether the goals of our ministry to families are too idealistic. They might even conclude that sexual purity can only be achieved in a protected environment. If those are your thoughts, then we need to tell you a little about Richard's background. That way you'll know that we're not saying this is an easy road to walk, but that it *can* be walked.

There's a beautiful irony in God's choice of our family to model this concept. First of all, as African-Americans, we're part of a larger community that is suffering from the consequences of sexual promiscuity even more acutely than our society as a whole. Second, Richard's personal background is one that from a natural viewpoint might have provided the *least* likely environment for maintaining high standards in sexuality as well as in other areas.

Yet Richard's desire to remain sexually pure, and his awareness of just how difficult that can be, began long ago in his own childhood. When Richard was ten years old, his father left his family, so he was without a dad for the rest of his life. At age thirteen the family moved to a poor urban area, where he was thrust into an environment of gang violence. Many of the young men he grew up with are now either dead or in prison for life.

Thus Richard already had two tough strikes against him as he entered adolescence. But he had known the Lord since he was three years old, and he was still walking with Him. So he had to learn how to live the Christian life daily in a hostile environment.

No doubt Richard had at least as many obstacles to emotional and spiritual health as most other people. But he remained sexually pure.

When we met and married, we resolved by God's grace to give our own children the best home, and the best chance at personal wholeness, that we could offer. Often in our earlier years as parents, we wrestled to provide our little ones with the kind of parental models we never had ourselves. We had few patterns to go by as we struggled to forge godly relationships with our children.

In other ways as well, our years as a family have not always been easy. We haven't always lived in the circumstances most conducive to maintaining a standard of righteousness. We've known at times, for example, the pressures brought on a home by a low income. And our children's school environment hasn't always been ideal.

So you see, there's certainly nothing exceptional about our external circumstances that has made our children more likely than others to remain sexually pure. If God's grace in this area can be manifested in our family, it can happen anywhere.

Some people have said, "Well, Richard's a pastor, and they probably have perfect kids. They don't know what it's like to deal with *my* teen." But the truth is that we know what it's like to deal with a difficult child.

Tim was probably one of the most strong-willed children we've ever seen. He came into the world fighting, and his first word was "No!" Renée can recall many times when she and he were both crying: Tim, because he had been spanked repeatedly for misbehavior, and Renée, because she was so upset about having to spank him. But Tim's strong will is now focused on serving God, and he is one of the most solid Christians we know.

In Tim and in our other children, we've seen the faithfulness of God day after day. He has honored their covenants with Him by giving them the grace to walk without moral compromise before Him. And He can do the same for your children.

Their Freedom to Choose

We recognize, of course, that all children have the same free will their parents have. They can choose to disobey God, choose even to turn their backs on God altogether. That's the risk God takes every time He sends a newborn into the world. Evidently, in the Lord's eyes, a human being who can freely choose what's right is infinitely preferable to a robot that's programmed to do nothing else.

If even God won't dictate all our children's decisions, we dare not try to do that ourselves. At best, we can cooperate with His grace through prayer, responsible love, and daily reliance on His Holy Spirit for wisdom. If we do these things faithfully, then we've fulfilled our calling as parents before God—whatever the outcome of our children's lives.

Having said that, we still believe God has given us as parents a greater opportunity than anyone else to influence our children for *good*. So we urge you to consider the benefits of making a key talk part of your parenting strategy. If you're the parent of a child who's fast approaching the age of sexual awareness, and the two of you haven't yet talked about making a commitment to sexual purity, now is the time to make plans for taking that step. The simple approach outlined in this book should provide you with all the tips you need to make the night of your key talk a success.

We believe God has given us as parents a greater opportunity than any-one else to influence our children for good.

Beyond that special evening lies a lifetime of challenges for the young person you love. Are you willing to invest the time, energy, and determination required to become your child's advocate during the exciting years ahead? If so, we believe the practical insights in this book for the long-term strategy with your child will serve you well.

The key-talk covenant can become your teenager's springboard for moral excellence in a number of areas as you tackle the serious issues of life together. Remember: A child is the only known substance from which a responsible adult can be made. Patience, wisdom, commitment, self-control, integrity under fire—these are the qualities of a godly character that, once built into young souls, will provide a lifelong foundation for fulfilling the destiny God has chosen for them.

The Power and Authority of Righteousness

Throughout these pages, as you've read, we hope that one conviction has been made clear: We believe that a person's covenant commitment to God to maintain sexual purity results in a unique grace, authority, and power to honor God with his or her sexuality, and to influence others in that direction. In a phrase, goodness is stronger than wickedness.

The Bible says that "righteousness will be the scepter of [God's] kingdom" (Heb. 1:8 NIV). A king's scepter represents his royal authority and power. So we conclude that this verse tells us God's authority and power reside in the people who practice His righteousness.

As long as the statistics about sexual activity among church youth remain the same as those for youth outside the church, their influence on their peers will be minimal. But if young Christians of this generation can understand who they are in Christ and can have a testimony of sexual purity among their peers, they will be able to speak to their world about holiness with a credible and convincing voice. God's grace, power, and authority will be evident in them.

When Jonathan was a high school junior, he stood before an assembly of younger teens and shared his testimony about the key-talk covenant. He's not by any means a shy person, yet we were amazed at the confidence and poise he displayed as he told those children in firm but loving terms their need to walk in purity before God. The young audience, typically restless and distracted, sat totally hushed as Jonathan told them about God's standards and his own dogged determination to keep them.

Why were those children so captivated by what our son had to say? We don't believe it was simply their strong interest in the subject matter. On the faces of the audience we could see respect—respect for the moral power that resonated in his voice. Jonathan could speak to them with credibility and authority because he spoke from a pure heart.

That day, many of those young people made their own commitment to walk with God and to take a stand for sexual integrity. Our prayer is that their parents will follow up their commitments with the kind of support that will see them safely through the temptations that lie ahead. If they do—and if thousands of parents across this nation do the same—our children could become the catalysts for a moral revolution with the power to transform our society, and indeed the whole world.

Points to Remember

- Sexual purity is not an unrealistic goal, nor is it achievable only in a protected environment. Many people who have made a covenant with God to abstain from sex until marriage, even under the greatest of pressures to compromise, have kept their promise to God.

- Children have a free will, and in the final analysis, we cannot make their decisions for them. But we can provide them with a healthy environment for choosing to walk with God.

- A covenant commitment to God to maintain sexual purity results in a unique grace, authority, and power to honor God with one's sexuality, and to influence others in that direction.

Key Scriptures

The lust of the eye leads to impurity
1. 2 Samuel 11:2–4
2. Job 31:1
3. Matthew 5:28
4. 1 John 2:16

Yielding to temptation
1. James 1:13–15
2. 2 Peter 2:18
3. Genesis 3:6
4. 1 Kings 11:1–4

Resisting temptation
1. Proverbs 1:10
2. Proverbs 4:14
3. Romans 6:13
4. Ephesians 6:13

5. 2 Peter 3:17
6. Proverbs 6:20–32

Abstain from sexual impurity
1. Matthew 5:28
2. Romans 1:24, 6:19
3. Ephesians 4:19
4. Colossians 3:5
5. 1 Thessalonians 4:7
6. Hebrews 13:4
7. 2 Peter 2:10

Abstain from fornication
1. Matthew 5:32
2. Acts 15:29
3. 1 Corinthians 5:1, 6:18, 7:2, 10:8
4. Ephesians 5:3
5. Colossians 3:5
6. 1 Thessalonians 4:3

Abstain from lasciviousness (lewd, lustful, wanton behavior)
1. Numbers 25:1–8
2. John 8:3–11
3. Romans 1:26–27
4. 1 Corinthians 5:1–2
5. 2 Corinthians 12:21
6. Ephesians 4:17–19
7. Jude 7

Covenant-keeping God
1. Deuteronomy 7:9
2. Genesis 9:16

3. Isaiah 54:10
4. Isaiah 55:3
5. Psalm 89:28–34

Reward of keeping a covenant with God

1. Exodus 19:5
2. Psalm 103:17–18
3. Psalm 132:12
4. 2 Thessalonians 3:3
5. Luke 19:17
6. Revelation 2:10

Examples of godly young people

1. Genesis 41:38, 46
2. 1 Samuel 2:26, 3:1
3. 1 Samuel 17:33, 37
4. 2 Chronicles 24:1–2
5. 2 Chronicles 34:1–3
6. Luke 2:49
7. 2 Timothy 1:5, 3:15
8. Ruth 1:6
9. Esther 4:16
10. Luke 1:38
11. Luke 10:39
12. Acts 21:9

Is homosexuality a sin?

1. Leviticus 18:22
2. Genesis 19:1–25
3. Judges 19:13–20, 48
4. Leviticus 20:13
5. Romans 1:26–32
6. 1 Corinthians 6:9

    7. Deuteronomy 23:17
    8. Jude 7

Is there hope for a homosexual?
    1. 1 Corinthians 6:9–11
    2. Galatians 6:7–8
    3. John 15:3
    4. Acts 10:34–35
    5. Titus 2:11–12
    6. Isaiah 43:25
    7. Isaiah 44:22
    8. Isaiah 55:7
    9. Micah 7:18
   10. 1 John 1:9

Reasons to avoid any type of premarital sex
    1. 1 Thessalonians 4:3–8
    2. Ephesians 5:3–5
    3. 1 Corinthians 6:9–20
    4. Colossians 3:5–6
    5. Ezra 18:20
    6. Romans 6:23

Recommended Resource List

AIDS and the Education of Our Children. U.S. Department of Education, 1988.

Boundaries in Dating, Henry Cloud & John Townsend, Grand Rapids: Zondervan, 2000.

Children at Risk, James Dobson & Gary L. Bauer, Waco, Tex.: Word Incorporated, 1990.

Christ Esteem, Don Matzat, Eugene, Ore.: Harvest House Publishers, 1990.

Girl Scouts Survey on the Beliefs and Moral Values of America's Children. New York: Girl Scouts of the United States of America, 1990.

Growing a Healthy Home, Mike Yorkey, Ed., Brentwood, Tenn.: Wolgemuth and Hyatt Publishers, 1990.

How to Help Your Child Say "No" to Sexual Pressure, Josh McDowell, Waco, Tex.: Word Incorporated, 1987.

How Will I Tell My Mother, Jerry Arterburn, Nashville: Oliver Nelson, 1988.

I Don't Want Your Sex for Now, Miles McPherson, Minneapolis: Bethany House Publishers, 2001.

Keeping Your Teen in Touch With God, Dr. Robert Laurent, Elgin, Ill.: David C. Cook Publishing Co., 1988.

Looking for Love in All the Wrong Places, Joe White, Wheaton, Ill.: Tyndale House Publishers, 1991.

Mothers and Daughters, Marie Chapian, Minneapolis: Bethany House Publishers, 1988.

Parenting Isn't for Cowards, Dr. James Dobson, Waco, Tex.: Word Incorporated, 1987.

Preparing for Adolescence: Straight Talk to Teens and Parents, Dr. James Dobson, Ventura, Calif.: Regal Books, 1978.

Questions Teenagers Ask About Dating and Sex, Barry Wood, Old Tappan, N.J.: Fleming H. Revell Co., 1981.

The Search for Significance, Robert S. McGee, Houston: Rapha Publishing, 1985.

Sex Has a Price Tag, Pam Stenzel & Crystal Kirgiss, Grand Rapids: Zondervan, 2003.

Sex Respect: The Option of True Sexual Freedom—A Public Health Guide for Parents, Coleen Kelly Mast, Bradley, Ill.: Respect, Inc., 1986.

Single Mothers Raising Sons, Bobbie Reed, PhD, Nashville: Thomas Nelson Publishers, 1988.

Single Parenting, a Wilderness Journey, Robert G. Barnes, Jr., Wheaton, Ill.: Tyndale House Publishers, 1987.

Successful Stepparenting, David J. Juroe and Bonnie B. Juroe, Old Tappan, N.J.: Fleming H. Revell Co., 1983.

Ten Mistakes Parents Make with Teenagers (and How to Avoid Them), Jay Kesler, Brentwood, Tenn.: Wolgemuth and Hyatt Publishers, 1988.

The Wonder of Me: Fertility Appreciation for Adolescents and Parents, Ruth S. Taylor, MD, MPH and Ann Nerbun, RN, MSN, Sumter, S.C.: Development and Enrichment Programs for Parents and Adolescents, 1990. *The Wonder of Me* is not available in bookstores. Request copies from For Wedlock Only or DEPPA, P.O. Box 383, Sumter, S.C. 29151.

Dr. Richard Durfield is a psychologist, award-winning author, educator, and international speaker. He is the creator of the Purity Key Talk, a youth abstinence program in which countless teens have enjoyed personal success while confronting sexual pressures. He and his wife, Renée, founded All About Marriage (www.allaboutmarriage.com), providing resources and seminars on cutting-edge strategies for marital stability and effective communication.

Dr. Durfield holds a PhD in Marriage and Family Studies from the Fuller Graduate School of Psychology, and has been licensed as a marriage and family therapist in two states. He completed advanced studies in Marital Therapy at the Gottman Institute in Seattle, Washington. He is a Certified Family Life Educator (CFLE) through the National Council on Family Relations and has received additional certifications as a JPEA Consultant, D.I.S.C. Consultant, Prepare/Enrich Consultant, and PREP Consultant. Richard recently retired from his position as an associate professor at Azusa Pacific University.

Renée Durfield is a bestselling author and popular speaker and has been an authority on family matters for the past thirty years. Renée travels extensively throughout the world, presenting proven solutions on marriage, parenting, teen sexuality, gender roles, and self-esteem issues. Renée and Richard offer marriage seminars throughout the year.

The Durfields live in southern Nevada, where they recently celebrated their fortieth anniversary. To reach them, please contact: All About Marriage, 2300 W. Sahara Avenue, Suite 800, Las Vegas, NV 89102, (866) 302-7567, (702) 982-7888 fax.